FULL SPECTRUM

Prints from the Brandywine Workshop

FULL SP

Prints from the Brandywine Workshop

Organized by Shelley R. Langdale

Essay by Ruth Fine

With contributions by Allan L. Edmunds and Shelley R. Langdale

Philadelphia Museum of Art

Published on the occasion of the exhibition *Full Spectrum: Prints from the Brandywine Workshop*, Philadelphia Museum of Art, September 7–November 25, 2012

The exhibition was funded in part by The Pew Charitable Trusts.

The catalogue was made possible by The Andrew W. Mellon Fund for Scholarly Publications at the Philadelphia Museum of Art.

Produced by the Publishing Department
Philadelphia Museum of Art
Sherry Babbitt
The William T. Ranney Director of Publishing
2525 Pennsylvania Avenue
Philadelphia, PA 19130-2440 USA
www.philamuseum.org

Art photography by Jason Wierzbicki
Edited by Kathleen Krattenmaker
Production by Richard Bonk
Designed by Lisa Benn Costigan
Printed and bound in Canada by
Transcontinental Litho Acme, Montreal

Cover: detail of *Night Flight*, by James Brantley, 1994 (see plate 11); pp. 2–3: detail of *Promise Land*, by Willie Birch, 1985 (see plate 9)

Note: All the prints illustrated in this catalogue were printed and published by the Brandywine Workshop and are a gift of the Brandywine Workshop, Philadelphia, in memory of Anne d'Harnoncourt, to the Philadelphia Museum of Art, unless otherwise stated.

PHOTOGRAPHY CREDITS
Hannibal Collins: p. 8; Allan L. Edmunds: figs. 13, 15; Kenley Gardner: fig. 1; Constance Mensh: fig. 20; James O'Neal: figs. 6, 7, 12, 14, 16, 17; Bill Peronneau: figs. 8–10; James Pounds: figs. 2, 3; Donnie Roberts: figs. 11, 19; Jason Wierzbicki: plates 1–100

Library of Congress Cataloging-in-Publication Data

Philadelphia Museum of Art.
  Full spectrum : prints from the Brandywine Workshop / organized by Shelley R. Langdale ; essay by Ruth Fine ; with contributions by Allan L. Edmunds and Shelley R. Langdale.
     pages cm
  Published on the occasion of the exhibition Full Spectrum: Prints from the Brandywine Workshop, Philadelphia Museum of Art, September 7–November 25, 2012.
  Includes bibliographical references.
  ISBN 978-0-87633-237-5 (PMA)
  ISBN 978-0-300-18548-5 (Yale)
  1. Brandywine Workshop—Exhibitions. 2. Prints, American—Pennsylvania—Philadelphia—20th century—Exhibitions. 3. Prints, American—Pennsylvania—Philadelphia—21st century—Exhibitions. 4. Prints—Pennsylvania—Philadelphia—Exhibitions. 5. Philadelphia Museum of Art—Exhibitions. I. Langdale, Shelley R. II. Fine, Ruth, 1941- III. Edmunds, Allan L. IV. Title.
  NE539.B73A4 2012
  769.9748'1107474811—dc23
               2012027026

CONTENTS

In memory of master printer
Robert W. Franklin, 1930–2012

Foreword

In any account of American printmaking in the second half of the twentieth century, the role played by organizations such as Brandywine Workshop must loom large. Studio, Collaborative, Press, Workshop: although the names given to the many new printmaking enterprises founded in the 1960s and early 1970s throughout the United States were as various as the ways in which they operated or the specific printing methods they favored, this should not be allowed to obscure the shared sense of purpose that led to their creation and proved to be an important factor in their success.

A key goal of this movement, if it may be called that, was to revitalize the practice of printmaking in this country and bring it into lively conversation with contemporary art in other mediums. This required significant change, most notably in the ways that prints were made and distributed, as well as a sustained commitment to technical innovation and experimentation in a field that still clung to time-honored traditions. As the course of American art changed radically in the decades after World War II, educator-entrepreneurs (for they were really both), such as June Wayne at the Tamarind Lithography Workshop and Kenneth Tyler at Gemini G.E.L., to their credit forced American printmaking to change in ways that reenergized the field and set a new course for the continued development of this venerable yet still vital medium.

Allan L. Edmunds and his life's work, Philadelphia's own Brandywine Workshop, founded in 1972, deserve far more than a special mention in this context. The workshop's focus from the beginning on serigraphy as a printmaking method, and its later use of offset lithography, was distinctive and warrants further study. Equally distinctive, and wholly admirable, was the commitment that Edmunds made early on to education and the active role he believed Brandywine Workshop should play in community engagement. Perhaps most important, he has pursued the ideal of printmaking as a fundamentally democratic process, one that by its very nature offers the opportunity for many different voices to be heard.

This catalogue and the exhibition it accompanies acknowledge and celebrate the Brandywine Workshop's donation of one hundred prints to the Philadelphia Museum of Art in memory of its late director Anne d'Harnoncourt. We are honored by this very special gift and are happy to have worked so closely with Allan on the exhibition and the many programs that will coincide with it. The spirit of collaboration that has animated his organization since its founding has been amply evident in the work we have done together to develop this project. It is our great pleasure to recognize Allan and the many artists, printers, and supporters whose collective efforts comprise the history of the Brandywine Workshop on the occasion of its fortieth anniversary.

I am delighted, as well, to have the opportunity to express my deepest thanks to The Pew Charitable Trusts and The Andrew W. Mellon Foundation, which so generously supported the exhibition and catalogue, and to the many individuals who helped to bring them about—most notably, Ruth Fine, former Curator of Special Projects in Modern Art at the National Gallery of Art, Washington, D.C., and a widely acknowledged authority on modern prints and drawings, for the wonderful essay she contributed to this publication, and Shelley R. Langdale, Associate Curator in our Department of Prints, Drawings, and Photographs, who organized the exhibition and oversaw the catalogue with her characteristic thoroughness, sharp intelligence, and good cheer.

Timothy Rub
The George D. Widener Director and Chief Executive Officer, Philadelphia Museum of Art

Brandywine Workshop: Four Decades

The board, staff, and Friends of Brandywine Workshop are grateful to the Philadelphia Museum of Art for its presentation of *Full Spectrum* and for recognizing the workshop's success at the moment we celebrate our fortieth anniversary. We are also indebted to the many individuals and art partners who participated in our planning committee to ensure that a wide range of communities benefit from the collaboration in educational outreach and the exhibition's traveling component.

Over the past several years it has been my personal pleasure to work with catalogue essayist Ruth Fine, exhibition organizer Shelley Langdale, Innis Shoemaker and John Ittmann of the Department of Prints, Drawings, and Photographs, and, more recently, Cheryl McClenney-Brooker, Joseph Meade, Jr., Barbara Bassett, Jean Woodley, and numerous other members of the Museum staff, past and present, across several departments. The effort to realize late director Anne d'Harnoncourt's proposal—in response to Brandywine's wish to give a significant number of prints to the Museum—of an exhibition of the workshop's prints could not have moved forward without the strong support and endorsement of the present director and chief executive, Timothy Rub. The Brandywine Workshop is grateful for his leadership and hopes to continue to be a partner in future programming.

Full Spectrum recognizes Brandywine Workshop and our mission to present opportunities for artists who face barriers of geographic location, or of social or economic factors, and also honors the many artists who have authored its vision and were crucial to its sustainability. Benny Andrews, Camille Billops, Robert Blackburn, Samuel J. Brown, John E. Dowell, Jr., Sam Gilliam, Paul F. Keene, Jr., Samella Lewis, E. J. Montgomery, Keith Morrison, John T. Scott, and Bernard Young are the spiritual force behind the organization and have provided a model for quality and integrity, without which an institution cannot prosper. As Brandywine Workshop continues to pursue its institutional aspirations, it will rely on collaborations and partnerships, connecting its legacy with that of others for a wider impact.

The exhibition and this catalogue examine the multiple forces and circumstances that allow art-making to thrive at a particular time and in a particular place. The prints represented here were created during a relatively brief period in the postmodern era of art history, when fine art printmaking experienced a particularly broad appeal among ethnic minorities and technical processes and social attitudes about the role of art in the wider community were evolving. New approaches to the creation and presentation of art (multimedia, digital, installation, and performance, among others) were also developing, expanding the range of artists and audiences who practice and engage in the conversation about art and underscoring its value within a more diverse society. Through its presentation of a wide variety of artists and backgrounds, styles and techniques, *Full Spectrum* functions as a survey of an exciting time in the long history of printmaking in Philadelphia and in the nation as a whole.

Allan L. Edmunds
Founder and Director, Brandywine Workshop

Artist Leon Hicks, founder Allan L. Edmunds, and intern James Miller at the Brandywine Workshop, Philadelphia, 1975

Apprentice printer Veronica Hanssens, director Allan L. Edmunds, and intern Gustavo Garcia review a print in process in the press room of Brandywine Workshop, 2012

EDUCATION AS ACTIVISM: CONVERSATION IN PRINT

Ruth Fine

Activities at Philadelphia's Brandywine Workshop, founded in 1972 as the Brandywine Graphic Workshop, are rooted in conversation, the kind of conversation that asks questions.[1] This exchange is an integral part of the workshop's three-part mission, which is to create works of art, to make connections between people from diverse and often international backgrounds, and to offer community-based educational opportunities. The questions that the Brandywine Workshop has raised over its forty-year history have addressed the potentially thorny matter of how to succeed simultaneously in all these activities at the highest and most broadly meaningful levels.[2]

Throughout the Brandywine Workshop's four decades, the roles that aesthetic position, ethnicity, gender, generation, politics, philosophical content, and technical experimentation play in the making of art have been central to the conversation, always under the tutelage of the workshop's founding director and guiding spirit, Allan L. Edmunds. A native Philadelphian, Edmunds was born in 1949 to Gerald Edmunds, who worked for the United States Postal Service, and Fannie (née Hairston), a homemaker kept busy raising Allan and his five siblings. All but one of the Edmunds children attended art classes, traveling from their home in West Philadelphia to study painting and drawing at the Philadelphia Board of Education–sponsored School Art League classes held on Saturday mornings at the Samuel S. Fleisher Art Memorial in South Philadelphia.[3] Allan made this weekly journey to Fleisher from the sixth through the twelfth grade

(he attended Overbrook High School), an experience that undoubtedly contributed to his later decision to pursue a profession in the arts. His first love, however, was mathematics, a discipline that leads to finite answers through a sequential process of problem solving. Edmunds's passion for this type of precise methodology has likewise been nourished in making prints at the Brandywine Workshop. "I love the process . . . [involving] a lot of steps," he has said. In addition, printmaking generally requires planning in advance and the ability to determine how to make adjustments when plans don't quite work out as anticipated. These are the aspects of the discipline that Edmunds cites when asked why he shifted from mathematics to printmaking.[4]

While Brandywine Workshop has focused primarily on printmaking, it has also embraced varied artistic expressions and mediums through activities that have included video and mural projects created with high school students (fig. 1), some of

Fig. 1. Members of the Nicetown Boys and Girls Club (now the Shane Victorino Nicetown Boys and Girls Club) working on a mural on Hunting Park Avenue, Nicetown, designed with John Queen and sponsored by Brandywine Workshop's Visual Artists in Public Service (VAPS) program, Philadelphia, c. 1979

the latter based on designs by internationally known artists, such as Jonas Dos Santos, Keith Haring, Jacob Landau, and the Cardiff (Wales) Mural Group, that were created for specific sites (see fig. 11). This volume highlights the workshop's primary practice—the creation of original works of art produced as editions (multiple original printed impressions of a specific image, each of them virtually identical).[5] At Brandywine Workshop this involves a collaborative process in which artists bring ideas to skilled artisans whose technical expertise helps them to realize their visions.

Historically, prints have championed the kinds of community interaction and discourse that Brandywine Workshop embodies. Printing and papermaking facilities established in Philadelphia already during the colonial period set the groundwork for the key role that printed images would play in local cultural history.[6] And Philadelphia's Print Club (now the Print Center), founded in 1915, was one of the first institutions in the United States to foster the

appreciation of prints as a fine art. Prints have also played a role in helping to spread literary as well as political and religious concepts, as documented, for example, in A. Hyatt Mayor's *Prints and People: A Social History of Printed Pictures* (New York Graphic Society, 1971). This widely admired text, published the year before Brandywine's inception, was an important influence on print aficionados of Edmunds's generation. In addition, in the wake of what has been called the printmaking renaissance of the 1960s, screenprinting and lithography—Brandywine's primary processes, with offset lithography being the current method of choice—as well as etching and woodcut have played central roles in the heady printmaking activity that has taken place internationally since that time.[7]

During his early career Edmunds, who holds undergraduate and graduate degrees in art and a certificate in art education from Temple University's Tyler School of Art, participated in the Print Club's groundbreaking educational outreach program Prints in Progress,[8] the initial iteration of which supported printmaking demonstrations in schools and community centers throughout the region. Over time this led to the creation of inner-city workshops that provided after-school and weekend printmaking programs. One of these was located in a two-story garage at 1923 Brandywine Street in the city's Fairmount section (not far from the Philadelphia Museum of Art), which would later become the Brandywine Workshop's first home (fig. 2).

Edmunds worked in the Print Club's Brandywine Street program for several months in 1971–72 in association with Marion Boulton Stroud, chairman of Prints in Progress, whom he calls its "driving force and spirit," and whose commitment to the program's graduates was one of the inspirations behind her founding of the renowned Fabric Workshop and Museum in Philadelphia in 1977.[9] Both the Brandywine Workshop and the Fabric Workshop build on the precedent of Philadelphia's Depression-era Works Progress Administration (WPA; later Work Projects Administration), specifically its Graphic Art Division, in which highly experimental printmaking approaches were explored. Local WPA participants included Dox Thrash, who contributed to the development of the richly tonal carborundum intaglio technique, and Sam Brown, who would become one of Edmunds's African American mentors.[10]

When Edmunds launched the Brandywine Workshop his commitments to educational programs, to community, and to artistic excellence through collaboration with international artists were already in place. The first two concerns had been fostered and encouraged by his large, closely knit African American family. Having grown up in a racially segregated neighborhood and having seldom traveled farther than a day's trip from Philadelphia, Edmunds attributes his aspirations

Fig. 2   Fig. 3

to international partnerships to his experiences during an undergraduate year at Tyler's school in Rome and his wanderings through Europe and North Africa that followed.

Also critical to his global outlook was Edmunds's introduction to Robert Blackburn, an African American artist a few decades his senior whose printmaking origins were rooted in the WPA's Harlem Community Art Center. In 1948 Blackburn, with the help of the painter and printmaker Will Barnet,[11] founded the Printmaking Workshop in Manhattan, to which artists from throughout the world gravitated.[12] Edmunds saw Blackburn's enterprise as "the model I [could] work from," but while he acknowledges the influence of the Printmaking Workshop, his own focus was different from Blackburn's emphasis on artists who would come to the shop to print their own editions. Edmunds was and remains more interested in sponsoring collaborations between artists and master printers in which the printer, through conversations with the artist, functions as a "facilitator between the ideas and the technology."

From the beginning, one of the Brandywine Workshop's principal concerns has been to engage African American artists. While Edmunds received strong support from white Temple University faculty, especially Richard Callner, director of the Tyler school in Rome, and his inspirational printmaking teacher Romas Viesulas, he attributes his belief in the possibility and survival of the Brandywine Workshop to successful black role models like Blackburn and Paul Keene (see plate 53), as well as others who are closer contemporaries, including John Dowell and Keith Morrison (fig. 3; see plates 19, 66, 67), the former of whom was the first African American to complete the prestigious Master

Printer Program at the Tamarind Lithography Workshop in Los Angeles. During his high school years Edmunds's philosophical foundation had been nourished by his awareness of anti–Vietnam War activism and by the emphasis within the Black Power movement on cultural nationalism. In founding the Brandywine Workshop in 1972, he followed precedents from the worlds of theater and dance—specifically Freedom Theatre and PHILADANCO, founded in Philadelphia in 1966 and 1970, respectively—and he embraced the ambitious aim of establishing a cultural institution that would enhance the artistic identity and awareness of his fellow African American artists, engaging with social and political issues that were important to them while collaborating as well with artists of other ethnicities.[13] Edmunds also wanted to work with existing art institutions throughout the city and to have the editioned prints produced at the workshop succeed within the wider artistic community. These were extraordinarily far-reaching goals for a twenty-two-year-old artist just embarking on his career.

Edmunds characterizes the year 1972 by the "energy stream circling around me." It was a critical time for him in several ways. In addition to the founding of the Brandywine Workshop, the year saw the inclusion of two of Edmunds's screenprints, *Strange Curiosities* and *Reflections on Silkscreen*, in the Philadelphia Museum of Art's landmark exhibition *Silkscreen: History of a Medium*, curated by Richard S. Field. Field commissioned the latter print for the show, and also had Edmunds print it in a poster version (one of three posters created by artists to celebrate the exhibition), a huge demonstration of institutional support for so young an artist.[14] Most important, however, this was the year Edmunds married Anne Pitts (fig. 4). The two had

Fig. 2. Louise Davis and Allan L. Edmunds at Brandywine Workshop, 1923 Brandywine Street, Philadelphia, winter 1972–73
Fig. 3. John Dowell playing a flute while working on a screenprint at Brandywine Workshop, 1975

Fig. 4

Fig. 5

met through his affiliation with Prints in Progress, where she was first the assistant to the director of the program and then the director herself. Over the years Anne Pitts Edmunds (now an arts management consultant) has remained a steadfast supporter of her husband's dreams and has encouraged and advised him, enhancing his efforts at building Brandywine Workshop through her love of art, artists, and community; her knowledge of nonprofit institutions; her fund-raising experience; and her willingness to shoulder much of the family's financial obligations (daughter Angela was born in 1977, Kimberly in 1981), enabling Edmunds to direct his earnings to the workshop's needs.

Brandywine Workshop started as a cooperative but was soon organized as a not-for-profit venture (incorporation took place two years after its founding, in 1974, an important step in Edmunds's aim to develop a viable cultural institution). Spearheaded by Edmunds, the enterprise was provided with modest financial and immense spiritual support from other Philadelphia-based artists, primarily African Americans, some of whom functioned as the workshop's first governing board. Among them were Brown and Keene, Janet Hoagland-Dailey, Leon Hicks, Libby Newman, Phyllis Thompson, David Stephens, John Wade, Clarence Wood, Bernard Young, and the photographers Gerald Carter, Bill Peronneau, and James Pounds. Like Edmunds, many of these artists also were public-school teachers. Edmunds paid the rent on the Brandywine Street space; Brown covered the telephone bill; and Hicks donated an etching press (which has

rarely been used). Stephens, who was on the staff at the Corcoran Gallery of Art, introduced Edmunds to Dowell and Sam Gilliam (see plates 33–36) at the opening reception for Dowell's 1971 solo exhibition at that Washington institution. African American artists with growing reputations, they would both become central to the Brandywine story. Wood connected Brandywine Workshop with the Philadelphia Museum of Art through his work with the latter's energetic Urban Outreach Program.[15] And Newman, a white artist, created the workshop's first edition, printed in 1973. Edmunds had met her through the Philadelphia chapter of the Artists Equity Association (fig. 5),[16] his membership in which speaks to his intuitive understanding of the importance of joining other art-oriented organizations to establish networking opportunities.

The Brandywine designation immediately linked the new printmaking enterprise to a recognizably Philadelphia-area context, in which the nearby Brandywine Valley has lent its name to a range of cultural institutions, including Brandywine River Museum, Brandywine Conservancy, and Brandywine Raceway (the first two are still in operation; the third closed in 1990). Screenprinting, also known as silkscreen or serigraphy, was the workshop's initial focus.[17] Multitasking was—and after four decades remains—the primary facilitator of its operations. While teaching high school art classes for thirty-five hours a week within the School District of Philadelphia's Parkway Program (one of the earliest alternative high schools in the United States to access community resources for learning), Edmunds created his own art at Brandywine Workshop in the evenings and on weekends (in 1972 he was preparing for his first solo exhibition at the University of Maryland, Baltimore

Fig. 4. Anne Pitts Edmunds and Allan L. Edmunds with the governor's wife, Ginny Thornburgh, at an installation of Brandywine Workshop prints at the Pennsylvania Governor's Mansion, Harrisburg, c. 1985
Fig. 5. Libby Newman, then chairwoman of the Artists Equity Association of Philadelphia, at an exhibition opening at the Philadelphia Civic Center Museum, c. 1973

Fig. 6

Fig. 7

County). And he also printed Newman's edition and others that were undertaken during the early years, for example those by Howard Watson, Wood, and Young. Most of Brandywine's efforts before 1975, however, supported the artistic under-takings of neighborhood teenagers, who had been introduced to printmaking by Prints in Progress during its time in the Brandywine Street space.[18]

Because of the limited availability of funds, all of Brandywine Workshop's early equipment was homebuilt. Fortunately, screenprinting requires only the most basic materials, so the initial needs were few: a framed, open-mesh screen, fluid inks, squeegees, and a clothesline and clothespins for hanging the printed sheets to dry. Although some of the early Brandywine screenprints used traditional cut lacquer-film and glue block-out stencils, the primary procedure followed at the workshop has been for artists to make color-separation drawings on frosted Mylar (a translucent plastic sheet) for transfer by means of light-sensitive materials, first to the printing screen and, in later years, to offset lithography plates (fig. 6).[19] Edmunds continued as the chief master printer through 1982, with occasional assistance from others.

To expand its reach beyond Philadelphia, Brandywine Work-shop began in 1975 to apply for funding from the Pennsylvania Council for the Arts (grantor of the workshop's first award of some $2,000), the National Endowment for the Arts (in both the Visual Arts and Expansion Arts programs), and other regional and national support groups, over the years receiving a number of grants and bringing several important political figures to the workshop, including Senator Edward Kennedy of Massachu-

setts and Joan Mondale, wife of the former Vice President and a strong advocate of the arts (fig. 7).[20] Also in 1975, Gilliam, an artist best known for his drape paintings, in which the canvas is freed from the confines of traditional stretchers, traveled from Washington, D.C., to be the workshop's first visiting artist-in-residence (see fig. 15). He has described the magical experience of making prints: "The medium itself stimulates.... It allows you to organize and watch the process while it is happening.... You see and hold onto an image step by step and can be taken over by the absorption of new ideas.... You aren't bound by any previous concepts."[21] While Gilliam had made prints at other workshops, he has emphasized the fundamental importance of Brandywine to artists whose reputations were less advanced than his and who thus had no other opportunities to pursue printmaking as a collaborative effort.[22]

Gilliam, one of few artists to have worked at Brandywine multiple times, also recalls the workshop's lack of sophisticated equipment at the time of his first visit, a topic of bemused con-versation years later about, for example, "the clothesline experience"—remembering his surprise that there was no commercial rack on which to dry his recently pulled prints. Indeed, such a rack, the workshop's first manufactured print-shop furniture, was purchased within a few days of his arrival. Gilliam's 1975 residency at the workshop coincided with the installation of his first outdoor public commission, *Seahorses*, on two exterior walls of the Philadelphia Museum of Art, as part of a festival put on by the Greater Philadelphia Cultural Alliance.[23] Such coordination with other institutions wove Brandywine Workshop's projects into the cultural fabric of the city. These types of alliances would multiply over the years (fig. 8).

Fig. 6. Howardena Pindell preparing her offset lithograph *Autobiography: Past & Present* (see plate 76) for color separation, Brandywine Workshop, 1988–89
Fig. 7. Joan Mondale, Philadelphia City Councilwoman Augusta A. Clark, and Allan L. Edmunds touring an installation at Brandywine Workshop's Kater Street location, 1982

Fig. 8
Fig. 9

Gilliam was followed as a Brandywine visiting artist by Romare Bearden in 1976. Among the most influential African American artists of his generation, Bearden was the initial recipient of the workshop's Van Der Zee Award (fig. 9), later renamed the Brandywine Achievement Award.[24] The original name honored the legendary Harlem-based photographer James Van Der Zee, who, along with Bearden, was an honorary member of Brandywine Workshop's board. Bearden and all subsequent award winners have been invited to make prints at Brandywine, in contrast to other artists who work there, who are selected through an application process overseen by a rotating Artists Advisory Committee, usually composed of three to five Philadelphia-based print practitioners. Members of the committee have included Dowell, Lois Johnson, and Hitoshi Nakazato, faculty members at Tyler School of Art, the University of the Arts (formerly the Philadelphia College of Art), and the graduate school of the University of Pennsylvania, respectively. The workshop's programs soon became widely known through the word-of-mouth enthusiasm of participating artists and, later, through Brandywine's many traveling exhibitions, of which the earliest was *Contemporary Print Images: Works by Afro-American Artists from the Brandywine Workshop*, widely circulated nationally by the Smithsonian Institution Traveling Exhibition Service starting in 1986. (Others, including shows circulated internationally by the United States Information Agency, are documented in this catalogue's chronology.) Moreover, with encouragement from Edmunds and other staff and supporters of Brandywine, applicants increasingly have come from a range of ethnic groups and have included a large component of emerging artists as well as mature practitioners with international reputations.

The Brandywine Workshop quickly outgrew its namesake facility, and in 1977 Edmunds purchased a four-story building at 1520–22 Kater Street in South Philadelphia, in part to house the workshop's many activities. The space was essentially a shell in need of total renovation before it could even begin to function as a print workshop—"and the neighborhood wasn't great either." But Edmunds saw potential in the site. As he observed, "it was only seven blocks from City Hall," and thus was located in the heart of the city. Edmunds believed change would come, and he was correct. Over the next three years, while doing much of the labor on the building himself, Edmunds focused the workshop's attention on educational programs, primarily through the federal government's Comprehensive Employment and Training Act (CETA), which funneled support through state and local channels to enable artists to do public service. Working with the Philadelphia Museum of Art, the Fleisher Art Memorial, and the Ile Ife Museum and Cultural Center (the first African American museum in Pennsylvania), among others, Brandywine co-sponsored workshops and lectures designed to expand the diversity of its constituents, both artists and audience. Although CETA funding for workshop projects ended around 1980, over the next several years, under a program Edmunds had named "Philly Panache,"[25] Brandywine continued its community-based undertakings and formed institutional connections on a project-by-project basis as funds were raised (fig. 10). "Philly Panache" attracted serious artists who were paid for their work while also performing public service. As ever, the goal was to find ways to

Fig. 8. Sam Gilliam, Anne d'Harnoncourt, and Clarence Wood at the Van Der Zee Award ceremonies held at the Philadelphia Museum of Art in October 1976
Fig. 9. Photographer James Van Der Zee (left) presents the Van Der Zee Award to Romare Bearden at the Philadelphia Museum of Art, October 1976

Fig. 10

bring art to inner-city, often disenfranchised neighborhoods. One success story still in place is the mural *We the Youth*, designed by Keith Haring and executed in 1987 on a wall at 22nd and Ellsworth Streets, in the city's Point Breeze neighborhood, by teenagers jointly sponsored by Brandywine Workshop and New York's CityKids Foundation (fig. 11). Over the decades, as Brandywine acquired more space, and as technology evolved and community needs changed, Edmunds initiated after-school programs in video and computer graphics for high school students.

The Kater Street print shop was ready for use in late 1979, and Chicago-based sculptor Richard Hunt (another Van Der Zee Award winner; see plate 48) was the first visiting artist to work there. Although screenprinting remained the technique of choice, by this time Edmunds was exploring the possibilities of offset lithography, which, like screenprinting, had its origins in the commercial world. He spent the next two years collaborating in this process with Dowell, using the offset press at a Center City lithography proofing shop owned by the family of Charles Gruman, one of Dowell's students at Tyler.

One advantage offset lithography has over screenprinting is that it offers the possibility of tighter "color registration"—the term applied to the accurate alignment of each of the colors used in a printed image. It also "uses a machine," as Edmunds puts it— shorthand for saying that a press facilitates printing at a much faster pace than screenprinting by hand allows.[26] With most Brandywine editions then, as now, numbering one hundred impressions plus twenty artist's proofs (editions were smaller and inconsistent in number when Brandywine first started), this speed would make a significant contribution to the workshop's creative endeavors, which increased during periods of high production from approximately a dozen screenprint editions a year to more than double that number with offset printing.[27]

By the close of 1982, Brandywine's Offset Institute, as it is called, was in action on Kater Street. In this case, the cutting-edge, experimental work in offset lithography undertaken in Philadelphia by the pioneering printmaker Eugene Feldman at his Falcon

Fig. 10. Participants, including many Brandywine Workshop artists, at a discussion following a lecture by the artist and scholar David C. Driskell at the African American Museum in Philadelphia, 1983. Seated at the table at the back are (from left to right) Robert Blackburn, Francisco Mora, Elizabeth Catlett Mora, David Stephens, Selma Burke, Ernest Crichlow, David C. Driskell, and John L. Wade (then chairman of Brandywine Workshop). At the left-hand table in the foreground are (clockwise from far left) Cheryl McClenney, Mary Schmidt Campbell, James Lesesne Wells, and Allan L. Edmunds.

Fig. 11. Philadelphia and New York high school students working on the mural *We the Youth*, designed by Keith Haring and sponsored by Brandywine Workshop in collaboration with CityKids Foundation of New York, at 22nd and Ellsworth Streets, Philadelphia, 1987. Keith Haring is seated on the scaffolding at lower left.

Press during the 1950s and 1960s provided a precedent, much as Blackburn's Printmaking Workshop in Manhattan had earlier.[28] At Brandywine Workshop two highly trained commercial printers, Jim (BJ) Hughes, followed by Robert W. Franklin (fig. 12), were retooled to work with artists, which requires a more subtle and complex array of interpersonal skills. Franklin, who recently passed away, was a Brandywine mainstay, not only as a printer but also as an all-around associate of Edmunds, contributing his essential historical memory of the workshop's activities.

Over time, Brandywine Workshop developed an additional commitment—to the maintenance of archival documentation about the careers of artists who have worked there. These records, as well as the workshop's growing inventory of prints and the commitment of gifts of prints and other materials from Robert Blackburn's estate and from the Hatch-Billops Collection (assembled by the theater historian James Hatch and the artist and filmmaker Camille Billops in New York), accelerated a need once again for additional space. In 1991 the workshop acquired an 1861 firehouse near Fitzwater Street on South Broad Street, Philadelphia's main north–south thoroughfare, which is referred to as the Avenue of the Arts because of the many cultural organizations that call it home (fig. 13). After two years of renovation,

Brandywine Workshop's educational activities moved to the new site in December 1993. As with the Kater Street facility, the print shop lagged behind, this time awaiting construction of a new building on a property adjacent to the firehouse. Meanwhile, the artists' work continued apace on Kater Street.

In addition to its archives and the print collection, the Firehouse Art Center, as it was named, housed Brandywine's lecture programs, classes for high school students, and the Printed Image Gallery, the workshop's first designated home exhibition space, something Edmunds had been coveting for nearly a quarter century.[29] Four years later, in 1997, the printmaking facility opened next door in a new building that also offered rental spaces for other cultural organizations. The Offset Institute's original single-color and two-color cylinder offset presses were replaced by a larger-format flatbed press that accommodates an expansive 38 by 50–inch sheet, a significant increase over the previous maximum of 22 by 30 inches. This press remains essential to the workshop's printing program. In Brandywine's current iteration, however, the Firehouse Art Center is no longer in operation, having closed for additional renovation in 2008, and yet another new life (independent of the Brandywine Workshop) has been proposed for its future. Thus all of the printing,

Fig. 12. Printer Robert Franklin at Brandywine Workshop's first offset press, at 1520–22 Kater Street, Philadelphia, 1986
Fig. 13. The Firehouse Art Center of Brandywine Workshop, 730–32 South Broad Street, Philadelphia, 1997

educational, archival, and exhibition activities now take place within the specially designed and constructed facility at 728 South Broad Street (see fig. 20).

Since 1972 close to three hundred artists from thirty-five states and fifteen countries have completed approximately eight hundred print editions at Brandywine Workshop, their conceptual reach reflecting the broad framework of contemporary artistic practice. Artists from Africa, Asia, and Latin America, and black, brown, and white artists from the United States, including participants of African, Latino, Asian, Native American (fig. 14), and European descent, all have worked there. Edmunds's lifelong connections within an African American network brought applications from within this community to Brandywine Workshop from the very start. By contrast, he has had to actively reach out to artists of other ethnicities, with word-of-mouth communications becoming an active force on the workshop's behalf in establishing these networks. In addition, lectures and exhibition programs at the workshop, as well as traveling shows, have helped to educate the broader public about art from various minority communities within the United States and internationally.[30]

In 1987 and 1988, for example, Brandywine Workshop joined with other Philadelphia institutions to host a lecture series about contemporary abstraction, which included a talk by Gilliam at the Pennsylvania Academy of the Fine Arts. These lectures were followed by a national series of panel discussions devoted to "African American Abstraction in Printmaking," which accompanied an eponymous exhibition that traveled to several U.S. cities, including Los Angeles, Newark (New Jersey), New Orleans, and Chicago. Other exhibitions and outreach programs have focused specifically on Asian and Asian American artists, Native American artists, and Latino artists.

Beginning in 1996, well before the current spate of cultural exchanges, Edmunds made several trips to Cuba with Ricardo Viera, a Cuban American artist and curator based at Lehigh University in Bethlehem, Pennsylvania, to speak about Brandywine's activities, introduce prints from the workshop to Cuban artists, and contribute to plans for the 2000 Havana Biennial. These trips preceded travel to the United States in 1999 by a group of Cuban artists, including Ibrahim Miranda (see plate 64),

Fig. 14. Hachivi Edgar Heap of Birds at work on his print *Telling Many Magpies, Telling Black Wolf, Telling Hachivi* (see plate 40), Brandywine Workshop, 1989

to work at Brandywine as well as at other art-school and university printmaking studios in the Philadelphia region. The following year, the exhibition *Hidden Images: Contemporary Cuban Graphic Art* was divided between Brandywine's Printed Image Gallery and Taller Puertorriqueño in North Philadelphia, with which the workshop had collaborated in 1986 to host the exhibition *Hispanic Artists Prints from Bob Blackburn's Printmaking Workshop, Inc.*

In the late 1980s and early 1990s, when funding was more readily available than it is today, as many as thirty artists a year participated in week-long Brandywine Workshop residencies. (That figure has now shrunk to ten or fewer residencies annually.) The relatively short duration of a standard Brandywine Workshop residency—one week—compared with those at other workshops, which tend to be considerably longer, is based on Edmunds's belief that many artists whose participation he wanted to encourage would not be able to spend more than a week away from their other, often income-producing, obligations. Such time limitations are experienced for a wide range of reasons—including race, ethnicity, age, gender, and experience—which makes Brandywine's commitment to working with artists from all backgrounds so exemplary. In this regard, the workshop's nonprofit stance has been essential. It is rare that a for-profit publishing workshop will invite artists to make prints without some belief in a potential market for the results. That market is dependent on the production of works by artists with established reputations, rather than the encouragement and promotion of young or under-appreciated practitioners that are part of Brandywine Workshop's practice.

In the effort to make its artists better known, the workshop has donated prints to several museums throughout the country, including the extensive gift to the Philadelphia Museum of Art of one hundred works to honor the memory of its former director Anne d'Harnoncourt that is documented in this catalogue.[31] The prints represented in the gift (see plates 1–100) emphasize the range of concerns expressed by artists at Brandywine Workshop, where the philosophical aim is to encompass nature and artifice, representation and abstraction, tradition and invention, and the complexities of a global artistic experience inclusive of marginalized communities. The diverse forms examined, the myriad images created, and the range of stylistic approaches that are embraced suggest today's many artistic possibilities. Identity and memory, political and social activism, relationships between art and history and art and society all enter into the visual conversation. As the artist and curator Margo Machida has rightly suggested, artistic discussion today "reveals the social and psychological tensions and ambiguities" within a broad "transcultural framework, as people, images, and ideas traverse porous national boundaries with increasing ease."[32]

The tension between abstraction and figuration that has dominated visual practice since the start of the last century is apparent throughout Brandywine Workshop's editions. Some of these, though abstractions, hint at the artists' embrace of visual elements rooted in nature (see plates 48, 92), while others offer no overt suggestion of sources in the visible world (see plates 12, 33). A visual element that runs through many of the prints is that of actual or implied collage (see plates 2, 76), emphasizing the important impact of the art of both Bearden and Robert Rauschenberg (Edmunds has cited the latter as his own major source of inspiration). In some instances, electronic and photographic manipulation, both of which are part of Brandywine Workshop's practice, expanded the use of two-dimensional collage by juxtaposing and resizing disjointed images and further altering relationships among them (see plates 39, 63). In others, the collage develops as a three-dimensional sculptural component (see plates 14, 43).

Several works combine screenprint and offset lithography (see plates 60, 70), while others confirm Brandywine Workshop's occasional use of other print techniques, such as woodcut (see plate 1). In one way or another, these works indicate the artists' essential attention to manipulating materials and forms. Other artists' prints emphasize figuration and elements of drawing, both to address narrative directions and to engage those political and social concerns that have been essential to conversation at the workshop since its founding (see plates 8, 90).

n 1997 Edmunds wrote a foreword for the catalogue accompanying the Brandywine Workshop exhibition *Inside/Out: Japanese and Japanese American Artist Prints*, in which he stated that the notion of Japanese and Japanese American art "assumes no defined sense of content, color, or composition that is indigenous to one culture, but mixes traditional values, modern art history, and training with themes of identity, social and environmental issues with purely aesthetic concerns."[33] The same could be said for most of the projects at Brandywine Workshop. By focusing on individual communities at specific times, the workshop has helped to teach us about "dislocations, and differences, as well as enduring and newly emerging connections," as recounted by Machida, the exhibition's guest curator.[34] The result is a richly nuanced collection of printed images. The selection documented here is layered in both physical and metaphysical ways that inspire us to broaden and also deepen a visual conversation that enables a better understanding of the world around us.

NOTES

1. According to an e-mail from Allan L. Edmunds to the author, January 26, 2012, Brandywine Graphic Workshop remains the official name, but Brandywine Workshop has been used since the mid-1980s to avoid confusion with Brandywine Graphics of Ardmore, Pennsylvania, a commercial company.

2. The most comprehensive study of Brandywine Workshop may be found in Halima Taha et al., *Three Decades of American Printmaking: The Brandywine Workshop Collection* (New York: Hudson Hills, 2004). Much of Brandywine's history is documented in more ephemeral materials in the workshop's archives, such as the newsletters, fund-raising brochures, and calls for visiting artist applications that have been issued (undated) intermittently over four decades. Many of the workshop's exhibitions were not accompanied by catalogues.

3. School Art League classes were held at several locations throughout the city in addition to Fleischer.

4. Allan L. Edmunds, videotaped conversation with the author at Brandywine Workshop, August 8, 2011, Philadelphia Museum of Art Archives. This conversation is the source for much of the information in this essay. Unless otherwise stated, all quotations are from this conversation.

5. Edition size is generally designated on each print as a fraction. For example, in an edition size of one hundred prints the works will be numbered individually, beginning with 1/100 and ending with 100/100.

6. William Rittenhouse and his son, Nicholas, founded the first paper mill in colonial North America around 1690 on Monoshone Creek, in historic Rittenhouse Town (as it came to be known), located along what is now Lincoln Drive in Philadelphia. For information on early Philadelphia printers, see Rosalind Remer, *Printers and Men of Capital: Philadelphia Book Publishers in the New Republic* (Philadelphia: University of Pennsylvania Press, 1996).

7. In the United States alone, starting with Universal Limited Art Editions in West Islip, New York, in 1957, and followed by Tamarind Lithography Workshop (now Tamarind Institute) in Los Angeles in 1960 (now based in Albuquerque, New Mexico), Crown Point Press in Berkeley in 1962 (now based in San Francisco), and Gemini G.E.L., also in Los Angeles, in 1966, dozens of print publishing workshops have opened their doors.

8. For a contemporary description of the Prints in Progress program, and of the Print Club in general, see John Canaday, "Obscure but Exemplary: The Philadelphia Print Club Is Little Known but Offers a Model for Effective Service to Art," *New York Times*, July 22, 1962.

9. See Marion Boulton Stroud et al., *New Material as New Media: The Fabric Workshop and Museum*, ed. Kelly Mitchell, exh. cat. (Cambridge and London: MIT Press, 2002).

10. For a comprehensive overview of Thrash and the role of the WPA program for printmaking in Philadelphia, see John Ittmann et al., *Dox Thrash: An African American Master Printmaker Rediscovered*, exh. cat. (Philadelphia: Philadelphia Museum of Art, 2002).

11. At the time, Barnet was teaching at the Art Students League and at Cooper Union in New York (he was appointed "league printer" at the former in 1935).

12. See *Creative Space: Fifty Years of Robert Blackburn's Printmaking Workshop*, Library of Congress, Washington, D.C., at http://www.loc.gov/exhibits/blackburn/overview.html (accessed March 2012), which celebrates the fiftieth anniversary of Blackburn's Printmaking Workshop.

13. Edmunds makes clear that in 1972 the conversation was about the black and white communities, without reference to artists of Latino or Asian descent, who later came to play an important role in Brandywine Workshop's commitment to inclusiveness.

14. The other two posters were made by Philadelphia-based Lois Johnson (born 1942) and British pop artist Edouardo Paolozzi (1924–2005).

15. The records of this program are stored in the Philadelphia Museum of Art Archives; see http://www.philamuseum.org/pma_archives/ead.php?c=COM&p=ifr.

16. Libby Newman was chairman, then president, of the Philadelphia chapter of the Artists Equity Association and, at the time Edmunds met her, also served as the governor's appointee on the Pennsylvania Council on the Arts.

17. Carl Zigrosser, the first curator of prints at the Philadelphia Museum of Art, originated the term "serigraphy" to distinguish fine art prints made by the

silkscreen process from commercial undertakings. The silk open-mesh fabric originally used to create the screens in this technique has generally been replaced by monofilament nylon, which is more durable and less expensive.

18. Although its location on Brandywine Street was short-lived, and the space was soon taken over by Brandywine Workshop, Prints in Progress workshops continued in other locations around the city, including on nearby Green Street. The program went through a number of iterations over the years, becoming independent of the Print Center around 1978 and ending in 1998.

19. For information regarding printmaking techniques, see Bamber Gascoigne, *How to Identify Prints: A Complete Guide to Manual and Mechanical Processes from Woodcut to Ink Jet* (New York: Thames and Hudson, 1986).

20. Mondale's visit was in 1982 and is referenced at http://news.google.com/newspapers?nid=2506&dat=19820715&id=5FJJAAAAIBAJ&sjid=1QkNAAAAIBAJ&pg=3319,3869249 (accessed March 2012). According to Edmunds (telephone conversation with the author on March 27, 2011), the reception at Brandywine Workshop in Kennedy's honor took place in 1995 and was organized by Congressman Chaka Fattah. The senator spoke briefly about the importance of the arts to American culture.

21. Sam Gilliam, in a telephone conversation with the author, January 8, 2012. By "step-by-step," Gilliam is referring to the proofing process, in which an image is printed at various stages in its development to produce sequential "state proofs," each of which documents the work at that specific moment.

22. Sam Gilliam, in conversation with the author, February 22, 2012.

23. According to Jonathan P. Binstock, *Seahorses* was reinstalled for a second time, in 1977, at the Brooklyn Museum, after which the ravages of outdoor display caused the drape painting to be retired; Binstock, *Sam Gilliam: A Retrospective*, exh. cat. (Berkeley: University of California Press; Washington, D.C.: Corcoran Gallery of Art, 2005), p. 104.

24. Other distinguished recipients of the Van Der Zee Award include Richard Hunt (1980), Elizabeth Catlett-Mora (1983), Gordon Parks (1990), Betye Saar (1992), Benny Andrews (1994), Barbara Chase-Riboud (1995), Moe Brooker (2003), Howardena Pindell (2005), and William T. Williams (2005).

25. Edmunds, assuming that "panache" would be unfamiliar to his constituents, hoped its use would be noticed and would suggest an attitude that embraced a sense of style and color and that would link the multiple activities of the workshop.

26. Edmunds, in conversation with the author, January 13, 2012.

27. Editions are evenly divided between the artist and Brandywine Workshop, which uses its share for donations to museum collections, inclusion in traveling exhibitions, and sales to raise funds to support its mission.

28. For a brief synopsis of Feldman's career, see *Philadelphia: Three Centuries of American Art*, exh. cat. (Philadelphia: Philadelphia Museum of Art, 1976), pp. 587–88 (entry by Ruth Fine Lehrer). Falcon Press closed following Feldman's death in 1975.

29. Prints had been exhibited in previous workshop spaces, as is evident, for example, in fig. 7, but never in a space designed for this purpose.

30. In 1976 the workshop also began to donate "satellite collections" of the prints produced on its presses to various public institutions and universities—often in memory of an artist, educator, or arts leader—to ensure wide access to the work of diverse artists. Recipients of these collections, ranging in size from a few dozen to several hundred prints, include the Smithsonian American Art Museum, Washington, D.C.; the Schomburg Center for Research in Black Culture, New York; Hampton University, Hampton, Virginia; Bennett College, Greensboro, North Carolina; Xavier University of Louisiana, New Orleans; the University of Delaware, Newark; the Philadelphia Museum of Art; and, most recently, Scripps College, Claremont, California (see also p. 77).

31. The one hundred prints that comprise the gift were selected by Innis Howe Shoemaker, John Ittmann, and Shelley Langdale of the Department of Prints, Drawings, and Photographs, Philadelphia Museum of Art.

32. Margo Machida, "(re)Turning Japanese," in *Inside/Out: Japanese and Japanese American Artist Prints*, exh. cat. (Philadelphia: Brandywine Graphic Workshop, 1997), p. 8.

33. Allan L. Edmunds, foreword to *Inside/Out*, p. 5.

34. Machida, "(re)Turning Japanese," in *Inside/Out*, p. 8.

1

Danny Alvarez (American, born 1964)
Untitled, 2006
Woodcut printed in black ink, and color offset lithograph, artist's proof
Image/sheet: 50 $^{13}/_{16}$ x 37 $^{1}/_{2}$ inches (129.1 x 95.3 cm)
Edition: 8 (color), 4 artist's proofs (color), 1 printer's proof (black and white)
Printer: Robert W. Franklin
2009-61-1

2
Emma Amos (American, born 1938)
Miss Otis, 2002
Color offset lithograph with collaged fabric border,
numbered 7/14
Image/sheet: 26 1/8 x 20 5/8 inches
(66.4 x 52.4 cm)
Edition: 14, 5 artist's proofs, 1 printer's proof
Printer: Robert W. Franklin
2009-61-2

3
Akili Ron Anderson (American, born 1946)
Kiss, 1995
Color offset lithograph, numbered 34/100
Image/sheet: 21 11/16 x 26 7/8 inches
(55.1 x 68.3 cm)
Edition: 100, 20 artist's proofs, 4 printer's proofs
Printer: Robert W. Franklin
2009-61-3

4
Benny Andrews (American, 1930–2006)
Amen Corner, 1985
Color offset lithograph, numbered 40/50
Image/sheet: 29 $^{15}/_{16}$ x 21 $^{7}/_{16}$ inches (76 x 54.5 cm)
Edition: 50, 6 artist's proofs, 2 printer's proofs
Printer: Robert W. Franklin
2009-61-4

5
Benny Andrews
Death, 1985
Color offset lithograph, numbered 44/44
Image/sheet: 30 x 21 $^{3}/_{4}$ inches (76.2 x 55.2 cm)
Edition: 44, 6 artist's proofs, 3 printer's proofs
Printer: Robert W. Franklin
2009-61-5

6
Rick Bartow (Native American, born 1946)
Segyp Kos'Ket Saw Tamp? (*Coyote Where Are You Going?*), 1997
Color offset lithograph, numbered 50/100
Image: 19 1/8 x 27 1/8 inches (48.6 x 68.9 cm)
Sheet: 20 3/4 x 28 7/8 inches (52.7 x 73.3 cm)
Edition: 100, 19 artist's proofs, 3 printer's proofs
Printers: James Hughes and Robert W. Franklin
2009-61-6

7
John Biggers (American, 1924–2001)
Family Ark, 1992
Color offset lithograph triptych; center panel, numbered 6/60; left and right panels, each numbered 94/100
Image/sheets (three joined): 29³/₈ x 49¹/₂ inches (74.6 x 125.7 cm)
Left panel (image/sheet): 29³/₈ x 13¹⁵/₁₆ inches (74.6 x 35.4 cm)
Center panel (image/sheet): 29³/₈ x 21⁹/₁₆ inches (74.6 x 54.8 cm)
Right panel (image/sheet): 29³/₈ x 13¹⁵/₁₆ inches (74.6 x 35.4 cm)
Multiple editions from variations of arrangements of the three printed sheets: 3-panel full-color version, edition of 100;
3-panel monochromatic version, edition of 100; center panel only, color version, edition of 60; diptych from two end
panels in monochrome, edition of 40, plus 4 artist's proofs
Printer: Robert W. Franklin
2009-61-7a,b (side panels); Purchased with the Print Revolving Fund, 1999-122-2 (center panel)

8
Camille Billops (American, born 1933)
The KKK Boutique, 1994
Color offset lithograph, numbered 50/100
Image: 23 ¹¹/₁₆ x 19 ¹/₁₆ inches (60.2 x 48.4 cm)
Sheet: 29 ⁷/₈ x 21 ⁵/₈ inches (75.9 x 54.9 cm)
Edition: 100, 20 artist's proofs, 6 printer's proofs
Printers: James Hughes and Robert W. Franklin
2009-61-8

9
Willie Birch (American, born 1942)
Promise Land, 1985
Color offset lithograph, numbered 62/70
Image: 21 ¹/₂ x 29 ³/₄ inches (54.6 x 75.6 cm)
Sheet: 21 ⁷/₈ x 29 ³/₄ inches (55.6 x 75.6 cm)
Edition: 70, 15 artist's proofs
Printers: James Hughes and Robert W. Franklin
2009-61-9

10
Sharon Bowar (American, born 1959)
Bloodroot, 1994
Color offset lithograph, numbered 50/98
Image/sheet (irregular): 21⁵/₈ x 29⁵/₁₆ inches
(54.9 x 74.5 cm)
Edition: 98, 10 artist's proofs, 4 printer's proofs
Printers: James Hughes and Robert W. Franklin
2009-61-10

11
James Brantley (American, born 1945)
Night Flight, 1994
Color offset lithograph, numbered 40/78
Image/sheet: 21¹¹/₁₆ x 27¹³/₁₆ inches
(55.1 x 70.6 cm)
Edition: 78, 6 artist's proofs, 3 printer's proofs
Printer: Robert W. Franklin
2009-61-95

12
Moe Brooker (American, born 1940)
And Then . . . You Just Smile, 2003
Color offset lithograph, numbered 32/38
Image/sheet: 21⁹/₁₆ x 21¹/₂ inches (54.8 x 54.6 cm)
Edition: 38, 2 artist's proofs
Printer: Robert W. Franklin
2009-61-11

13
Barbara Chase-Riboud (American, born 1939)
Akhmatova's Monument, 1995
Color offset lithograph, numbered 50/100
Image/sheet: 29⁷/₈ x 21⁵/₈ inches (75.9 x 54.9 cm)
Edition: 100, 6 artist's proofs, 4 printer's proofs
Printer: Robert W. Franklin
2009-61-12

14
Nannette Acker Clark (American, born 1948)
Untitled, 1992
Color offset lithograph paper construction, numbered 10/50
21 5/8 x 28 x 9/16 inches (54.9 x 71.1 x 1.3 cm)
Edition: 50
Printer: Robert W. Franklin
2009-61-13

15
Don Colley (American, born 1954)
Evangelismo, 1992
Color offset lithograph, numbered 42/100
Image/sheet: 21 13/16 x 30 1/16 inches (55.4 x 76.4 cm)
Edition: 100, 20 artist's proofs, 2 printer's proofs
Printers: James Hughes and Robert W. Franklin
2009-61-14

16
Joyce de Guatemala (Guatemalan, born Mexico, 1934–2000)
Beyond the Year 2000, 1993
Color offset lithograph and screenprint paper construction with
foam core board, numbered 14/72
21 5/8 x 30 1/16 x 1/2 inches (54.9 x 76.4 x 1.2 cm)
Edition: 72, 8 artist's proofs, 4 printer's proofs
Printers: James Hughes and Robert W. Franklin (offset lithograph)
and Allan L. Edmunds (screenprint)
2009-61-96

17
Louis Delsarte (American, born 1944)
Heaven and Earth, 1998
Color offset lithograph, numbered 50/100
Image/sheet: 21 $^{7}/_{16}$ x 28 $^{1}/_{8}$ inches
(54.5 x 71.4 cm)
Edition: 100, 20 artist's proofs, 4 printer's proofs
Printer: Robert W. Franklin
2009-61-15

18
Louis Delsarte
Unity, 1995
Color offset lithograph, numbered 50/100
Image/sheet: 28 $^{7}/_{8}$ x 21 $^{1}/_{2}$ inches
(73.3 x 54.6 cm)
Edition: 100, 20 artist's proofs, 4 printer's proofs
Printer: Robert W. Franklin
2009-61-16

19
John E. Dowell, Jr. (American, born 1941)
The Wonder, 2001
Color offset lithograph, numbered 12/40
Image: 17 1/16 x 19 7/8 inches (43.3 x 50.5 cm)
Sheet: 21 15/16 x 24 inches (55.7 x 61 cm)
Edition: 40, 8 artist's proofs, 2 printer's proofs
Printer: Robert W. Franklin
2009-61-17

20
James Dupree (American, born 1948)
Man, Mannequin, Manure, 1984
Color offset lithograph, numbered 44/100
Image/sheet: 22 1/4 x 30 1/16 inches
(56.5 x 76.4 cm)
Edition: 100, 24 artist's proofs, 2 printer's proofs
Printer: James Hughes
2009-61-18

21
Barbara Duval (American, born 1956)
Ingwer I, 1989
Offset lithograph, numbered 50/70
Image/sheet: 29 $^{15}/_{16}$ x 21 $^{1}/_{2}$ inches (76 x 54.6 cm)
Edition: 70, 10 artist's proofs
Printer: Robert W. Franklin
2009-61-19

22
Barbara Duval
Ingwer II, 1989
Offset lithograph, numbered 50/80
Image/sheet: 30 x 21 $^{1}/_{2}$ inches (76.2 x 54.6 cm)
Edition: 80, 12 artist's proofs
Printer: Robert W. Franklin
2009-61-20

23
Barbara Duval
Ingwer III, 1989
Offset lithograph, numbered 50/80
Image/sheet: 29⁷/₈ x 21¹/₂ inches (75.9 x 54.6 cm)
Edition: 80, 4 artist's proofs
Printer: Robert W. Franklin
2009-61-21

24
Barbara Duval
Ingwer IV, 1989
Offset lithograph, numbered 50/80
Image/sheet: 29⁷/₈ x 21¹/₂ inches (75.9 x 54.6 cm)
Edition: 80, 12 artist's proofs
Printer: Robert W. Franklin
2009-61-22

25
Allan L. Edmunds (American, born 1949)
Irving Fryar, 1997
Color offset lithograph, artist's proof
Image/sheet: 29 15/16 x 21 9/16 inches
(76 x 54.8 cm)
Edition: 100 (donated in full to the Philadelphia Eagles
Youth Partnership), 25 artist's proofs retained
by Brandywine Workshop
Printers: James Hughes and Robert W. Franklin
2009-61-23

26
Rodney Ewing (American, born 1964)
My Country Needs Me, 1996
Color offset lithograph, numbered 50/80
Image/sheet: 21 7/16 x 29 7/8 inches
(54.5 x 75.9 cm)
Edition: 80, 10 artist's proofs, 4 printer's proofs
Printer: Robert W. Franklin
2009-61-24

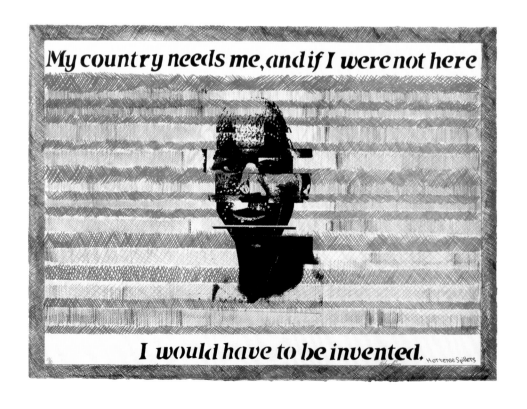

27
Vincent Falsetta (American, born 1949)
401-83, 1983
Color screenprint, numbered 36/45
Image/sheet: 29 $^{13}/_{16}$ x 22 $^{1}/_{4}$ inches
(75.7 x 56.5 cm)
Edition: 45, 8 artist's proofs, 3 printer's proofs
Printer: James Hughes
2009-61-26

28
Vincent Falsetta
Blue with Dog, 1989
Color offset lithograph, numbered 50/74
Image/sheet: 21 $^{5}/_{8}$ x 30 inches
(54.9 x 76.2 cm)
Edition: 74, 20 artist's proofs, 1 printer's proof
Printers: James Hughes and Robert W. Franklin
2009-61-25

29
Joseph Feddersen (Native American, born 1953)
Self-Portrait, 1989
Color offset lithograph, numbered 52/100
Image/sheet: 20^1/$_4$ x 29^1/$_2$ inches (51.4 x 74.9 cm)
Edition: 100, 20 artist's proofs, 2 printer's proofs
Printer: James Hughes
2009-61-27

30
Rafael Ferrer (Puerto Rican, born 1933)
American Dance Festival 1991, 1991
Color offset lithograph, working proof for poster
Image/sheet: 29^{15}/$_{16}$ x 21^7/$_{16}$ inches (76 x 54.4 cm)
Edition: 100 posters for Taller Puertorriqueño,
12 proofs retained by Brandywine Workshop
Printers: James Hughes and Robert W. Franklin
2009-61-28

31
Ruth Fine (American, born 1941)
Brandywine Garden, 1982
Color screenprint, numbered 50/50
Image (irregular): 22 x 14 1/8 inches (55.9 x 35.9 cm)
Sheet: 30 1/16 x 22 3/8 inches (76.4 x 56.8 cm)
Edition: 50, 10 artist's proofs, 1 printer's proof
Printer: Allan L. Edmunds
2009-61-29

32
Frank Galuszka (American, born 1947)
Flowers, 1994
Color offset lithograph, numbered 52/100
Image/sheet: 22 x 29 15/16 inches (55.9 x 76 cm)
Edition: 100, 20 artist's proofs, 4 printer's proofs
Printers: James Hughes and Robert W. Franklin
2009-61-30

33
Sam Gilliam (American, born 1933)
Harlem Nights, 1993
Color offset lithograph and screenprint collage, numbered 30/30
Image/sheet (irregular top edge): 27 1/2 x 34 11/16 inches (69.9 x 88.1 cm)
Edition: 30, 4 artist's proofs, 3 printer's proofs
Printers: Robert W. Franklin (offset lithograph) and Allan L. Edmunds (screenprint)
2009-61-31

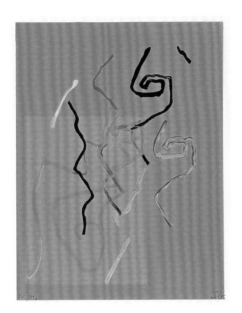

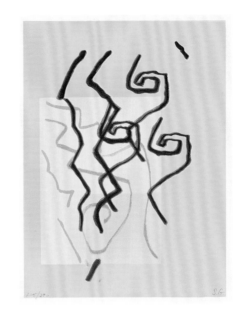

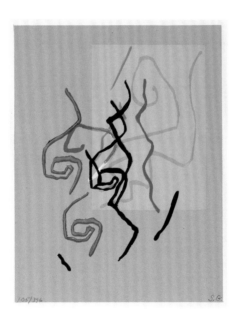

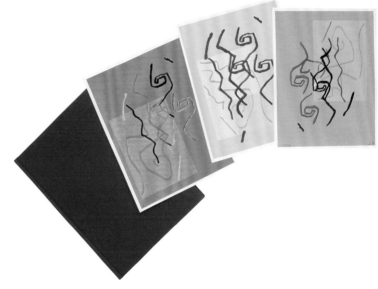

34–36
Sam Gilliam
Untitled (Red), *Untitled (Yellow)*, and *Untitled (Blue)*, 2004
Suite of three color offset lithographs, each numbered 105/396
Made for the deluxe edition of the book *Three Decades of American Printmaking:*
The Brandywine Workshop Collection (New York: Hudson Hills Press, 2004)
Each image, approximately: 10¹/₂ x 8 inches (26.7 x 20.3 cm)
Each sheet, approximately: 11 x 8¹/₂ inches (27.9 x 21.6 cm)
Book in slipcase: 12¹¹/₁₆ x 9¹/₂ x 1⁵/₁₆ inches (32.2 x 24.1 x 3.3 cm)
Edition: 396 (each)
Printers: James Hughes and Robert W. Franklin
2009-61-93a–d

37
Ricardo Gouveia (American, born 1966)
4% Off / 96% On, 1996
Color offset lithograph, numbered 50/90
Image/sheet: 29 $^{13}/_{16}$ x 21 $^{11}/_{16}$ inches
(75.7 x 55.1 cm)
Edition: 90, 6 artist's proofs, 4 printer's proofs
Printers: James Hughes and Robert W. Franklin
2009-61-32

38
Elizabeth Grajales (American, born 1952)
Watching, 1989
Color offset lithograph, numbered 50/100
Image/sheet: 21 $^{5}/_{8}$ x 30 inches
(54.9 x 76.2 cm)
Edition: 100, 20 artist's proofs
Printers: James Hughes and Robert W. Franklin
2009-61-33

39
Michael D. Harris (American, born 1948)
Mothers and the Presence of Myth, 1994
Color offset lithograph, numbered 50/100
Image/sheet: 29 $^{15}/_{16}$ x 21 $^{5}/_{8}$ inches
(76 x 54.9 cm)
Edition: 100, 20 artist's proofs, 4 printer's proofs
Printer: Robert W. Franklin
2009-61-34

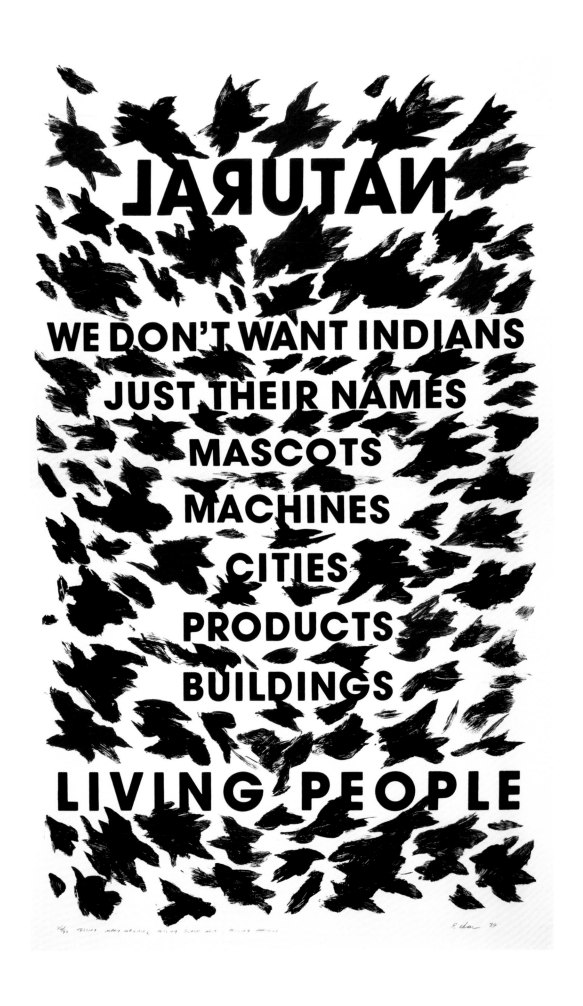

40

Hachivi Edgar Heap of Birds (Native American, born 1954)
Telling Many Magpies, Telling Black Wolf, Telling Hachivi, 1989
Screenprint, numbered 46/50
Image/sheets (two joined), approximately: 72 $^{15}/_{16}$ x 45 $^{1}/_{8}$ inches
(183.7 x 114.4 cm)
Edition: 50, 1 artist's proof
Printer: Franz Spohn
2009-61-35a,b

41

Barkley Hendricks (American, born 1945)
Sacrifice of the Watermelon Virgin or Shirt Off Her Back, 1987
Color offset lithograph, numbered 72/85
Image/sheet: 21 $^{3}/_{4}$ x 29 $^{15}/_{16}$ inches (55.2 x 76 cm)
Edition: 85, 1 printer's proof
Printer: Robert W. Franklin
2009-61-36

42

Curlee Raven Holton (American, born 1951)
Blind Spots, 2002
Color offset lithograph, numbered 40/40
Image/sheet: 24 $^{13}/_{16}$ x 21 $^{9}/_{16}$ inches (63 x 54.8 cm)
Edition: 40, 1 artist's proof, 2 printer's proofs
Printer: Robert W. Franklin
2009-61-37

43
Mei-ling Hom (American, born 1951)
Cross Cultural Pictograms, 1992
Color offset lithograph paper construction,
numbered 36/60
21 1/2 x 25 1/4 x 1 1/8 inches
(54.6 x 64.1 x 2.9 cm)
Edition: 60, 12 artist's proofs, 2 printer's proofs
Printer: Robert W. Franklin
2009-61-38

44
Richard Hricko (American, born 1952)
Nearing the Bridge IV, 1990
Color offset lithograph, numbered 50/100
Image/sheet: 29 3/16 x 19 1/4 inches
(74.1 x 48.9 cm)
Edition: 100, 12 artist's proofs, 2 printer's proofs
Printers: James Hughes and Robert W. Franklin
2009-61-40

45
Arlan Huang (American, born 1948)
Fish Tales, 1992
Color offset lithograph, numbered 50/50
Image/sheet: 21 11/16 x 30 1/8 inches
(55.1 x 76.5 cm)
Edition: 50, 10 artist's proofs, 2 printer's proofs
Printers: James Hughes and Robert W. Franklin
2009-61-41

46
Ed Hughes (American, born 1940)
Spring IV and *Spring III*, 2007
Color offset lithograph diptych, numbered 4/16
Image/sheets (two joined): 29 1/8 x 42 5/8 inches
(74 x 108.3 cm)
Edition: 16, 4 artist's proofs
Printer: Robert W. Franklin
2009-61-42a,b

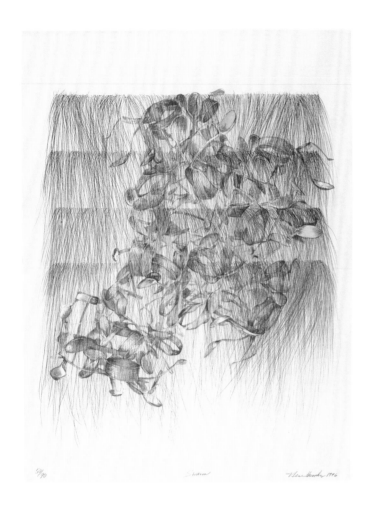

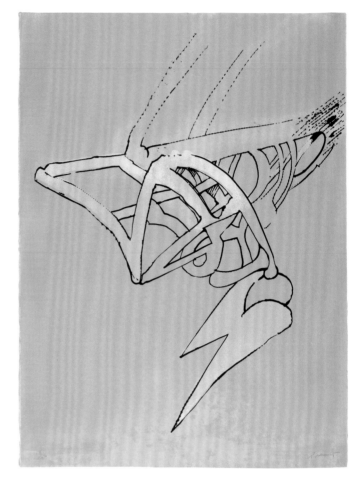

47
Nene Humphrey (American, born 1947)
Swarm, 1996
Offset lithograph in gray and brown inks,
numbered 50/70
Sheet: 29³/₄ x 22¹/₁₆ inches (75.6 x 56 cm)
Edition: 70, 8 artist's proofs, 2 printer's proofs
Printers: James Hughes and Robert W. Franklin
2009-61-43

48
Richard Howard Hunt (American, born 1935)
Untitled (Gray), 1980
Screenprint printed in black, gray, and pale yellow inks,
numbered 18/32
Image/sheet: 30 x 22³/₈ inches (76.2 x 56.8 cm)
Edition: 32, 2 artist's proofs
Printer: Allan L. Edmunds
2009-61-44

49
Frank Hyder (American, born 1951)
Primal Relation, 1992
Color offset lithograph, numbered 50/100
Image/sheet: 30 x 21 ¹³/₁₆ inches (76.2 x 55.4 cm)
Edition: 100, 20 artist's proofs, 2 printer's proofs
Printers: James Hughes and Robert W. Franklin
2009-61-45

50
Michi Itami (American, born 1938)
Mei, 1997
Color offset lithograph, numbered 50/100
Image: 20 ¹/₄ x 17 inches (51.4 x 43.2 cm)
Sheet: 29 ³/₈ x 21 ⁵/₈ inches (74.6 x 54.9 cm)
Edition: 100, 20 artist's proofs, 4 printer's proofs
Printers: James Hughes and Robert W. Franklin
2009-61-46

51
Wadsworth Jarrell (American, born 1929)
Tender Souls, 1995
Color offset lithograph, numbered 50/76
Image/sheet: 21 1/2 x 29 7/8 inches
(54.6 x 75.9 cm)
Edition: 76, 4 artist's proofs, 2 printer's proofs
Printers: James Hughes and Robert W. Franklin
2009-61-47

52
Martina Johnson-Allen (American, born 1947)
Another Realm, 2006
Offset lithograph printed in brown inks, numbered 50/88
Image/sheet: 21 7/8 x 27 1/16 inches
(55.6 x 68.7 cm)
Edition: 88, 10 artist's proofs, 3 printer's proofs
Printer: Robert W. Franklin
2009-61-97

53
Paul F. Keene, Jr. (American, 1920–2009)
Generations, 1996
Color offset lithograph, numbered 50/100
Image/sheets (two joined): 43 1/8 x 29 7/8 inches
(109.5 x 75.9 cm)
Edition: 100, 20 artist's proofs
Printer: Robert W. Franklin
2009-61-48a,b

54
Jacob Landau (American, 1917–2001)
Brandywine Impression (34th Psalm), 1988
Color offset lithograph, numbered 15/25
Image: 20 x 27 1/2 inches (50.8 x 69.9 cm)
Sheet: 22 x 29 15/16 inches (55.9 x 76 cm)
Edition: 25
Printer: James Hughes
2009-61-49

55
Jim Lee (American, born 1954)
Alchemical Lion, 1991
Accordion-bound book, ten panels
Color offset lithographs and computer-generated text, numbered 46/100
Book: 10 7/16 x 6 1/8 x 9/16 inches (26.5 x 15.6 x 1.4 cm)
Open/unfolded: 10 1/2 x 55 7/8 inches (26.7 x 141.9 cm)
Text by poet Jesse Glass; copublished by Blue Moon Press,
Glastonbury, Connecticut, and Brandywine Workshop
Edition: 100, 20 artist's proofs, 1 printer's proof
Printer: Robert Franklin
2009-61-50

56
Paul Pak-hing Lee (American, born Hong Kong,1962)
Untitled (Spent), 1998
Color offset lithograph, numbered 46/100
Image: 24 x 17 1/4 inches (61 x 43.8 cm)
Sheet: 30 x 21 3/4 inches (76.2 x 55.2 cm)
Edition: 100
Printers: James Hughes and Robert W. Franklin
2009-61-39

57
Hughie Lee-Smith (American, 1915–1999)
Actress, 1993
Color offset lithograph, numbered 90/100
Image: 26 x 20 inches (66 x 50.8 cm)
Sheet: 29 1/8 x 21 3/4 inches (74 x 55.2 cm)
Edition: 100, 16 artist's proofs, 3 printer's proofs
Printer: Robert W. Franklin
2009-61-78

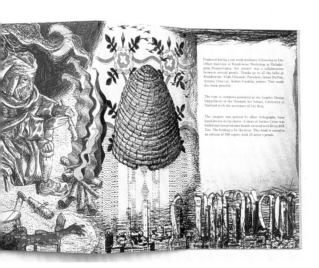

58
Samella Lewis (American, born 1924)
Boy on Bench, 2007
Color offset lithograph, numbered 26/26
Image/sheet: 27 1/2 x 20 3/8 inches (69.9 x 51.8 cm)
Edition: 26
Printer: Robert W. Franklin
2009-61-51

59
Leo Limón (American, born 1952)
L.A. Greenhouse Premiere, 1990
Color offset lithograph, numbered 50/100
Image: 21 11/16 x 29 15/16 inches (55.1 x 76 cm)
Sheet: 22 x 29 15/16 inches (55.9 x 76 cm)
Edition: 100, 20 artist's proofs, 1 printer's proof
Printer: Robert W. Franklin
2009-61-52

60
Alvin Loving (American, 1935–2005)
Mara C, 2003
Color offset lithograph and screenprint, numbered 12/20
Image/sheet: 27⁷/₈ x 21¹/₂ inches (70.8 x 54.6 cm)
Edition: 20
Printers: James Hughes (offset lithograph) and
Allan L. Edmunds (screenprint)
2009-61-53

61
Jack Malotte (Native American, born 1953)
Screaming Eagle Blues, 1989
Color offset lithograph, numbered 50/100
Image/sheet: 21¹/₂ x 29¹⁵/₁₆ inches (54.6 x 76 cm)
Edition: 100, 20 artist's proofs, 1 printer's proof
Printers: James Hughes and Robert W. Franklin
2009-61-54

62
Valerie Maynard (American, born 1937)
Send the Message Clearly (Full Color, A), 1992
Color offset lithograph, numbered 50/100
Image/sheet: 30 1/16 x 21 5/8 inches (76.4 x 54.9 cm)
Edition: 100, 16 artist's proofs, 2 printer's proofs
Printers: James Hughes and Robert W. Franklin
2009-61-55

63
Yong Soon Min (American, born South Korea, 1953)
Crossings, 1992
Color offset lithograph, numbered 48/58
Image/sheet: 30 1/16 x 21 9/16 inches (76.4 x 54.8 cm)
Edition: 58, 18 artist's proofs, 2 printer's proofs
Printer: Robert W. Franklin
2009-61-56

64
Ibrahim Miranda (Cuban, born 1969)
El túnel, 1999
Screenprint printed in light tan and black inks,
numbered 23/39
Image: 18 1/8 x 24 inches (46 x 61 cm)
Sheet: 21 13/16 x 27 1/2 inches (55.4 x 69.9 cm)
Edition: 39
Printer: Lois Johnson; printed at and copublished
with the University of the Arts, Philadelphia
2009-61-57

65
Evangeline Montgomery (American, born 1930)
Napa Weeds, 2006
Color offset lithograph, artist's proof
Image: 19 1/8 x 24 7/8 inches (48.6 x 63.2 cm)
Sheet: 22 1/8 x 29 3/4 inches (56.2 x 75.6 cm)
Edition: 14, 1 artist's proof
Printer: Robert W. Franklin
2009-61-58

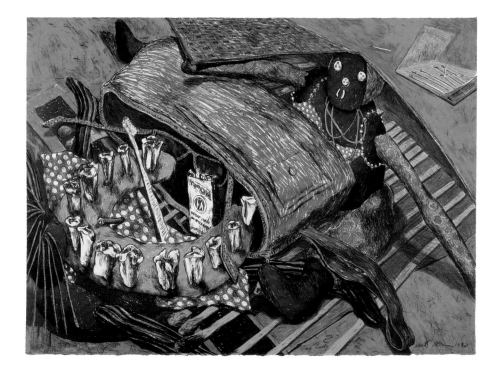

66
Keith Morrison (American, born Jamaica, 1942)
African Buns, 1993
Color offset lithograph, numbered 50/100
Image/sheet: 21 5/8 x 30 inches
(54.9 x 76.2 cm)
Edition: 100, 5 artist's proofs
Printer: Robert W. Franklin
2009-61-59

67
Keith Morrison
Bag Lady, 1993
Color offset lithograph, numbered 50/100
Image/sheet: 21 5/8 x 27 15/16 inches
(54.9 x 76 cm)
Edition: 100, 6 artist's proofs
Printer: Robert W. Franklin
2009-61-60

68
Hiroshi Murata (American, born Japan, 1941)
Hinode, 1986
Color offset lithograph diptych, numbered 50/72
Image/sheets (two joined): 29 5/16 x 42 3/4 inches
(74.5 x 108.6 cm)
Edition: 72, 1 printer's proof
Printers: James Hughes and Robert W. Franklin
2009-61-61a,b

69
Edith Neff (American, 1943–1995)
Elephant Ride, 1993
Color offset lithograph, numbered 54/70
Image: 21 11/16 x 26 1/16 inches (55.1 x 66.2 cm)
Sheet: 21 3/4 x 30 inches (55.2 x 76.2 cm)
Edition: 70, 1 artist's proof, 2 printer's proofs
Printers: James Hughes and Robert W. Franklin
2009-61-62

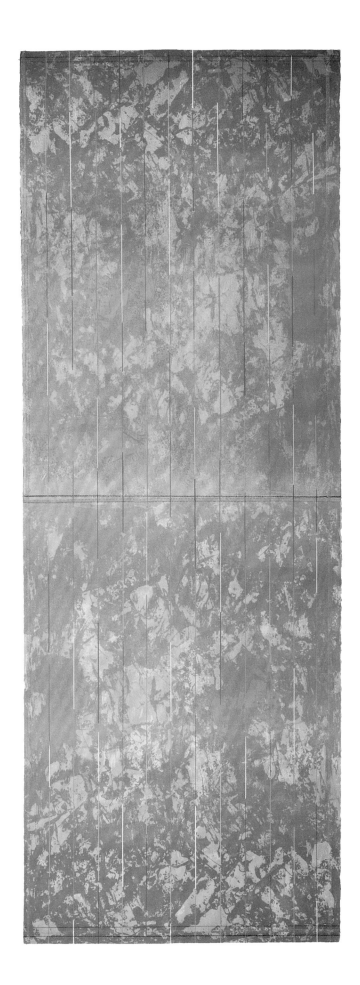

70
Kenneth Noland (American, 1924–2010)
Florida Shades, 1991
Color offset lithograph and screenprint with stitching in yellow
and pink threads, artist's proof
Image/sheets (two joined): 59⅝ x 21⁷/₁₆ inches (151.4 x 54.5 cm)
Edition: 75, 2 artist's proofs, 1 printer's proof
Printers: James Hughes and Robert W. Franklin (offset lithograph)
and Allan L. Edmunds (screenprint); stitching by technicians at the
Fabric Workshop, Philadelphia
Commissioned/published by the Boca Raton Museum of Art, Florida
2009-61-63

71
Helen Oji (American, born 1950)
Cultural Exchange, 1996
Color offset lithograph, numbered 50/100
Image: 16¹⁵/₁₆ x 23 inches (43 x 58.4 cm);
Sheet: 21³/₄ x 29⁷/₈ inches (55.2 x 75.9 cm)
Edition: 100, 20 artist's proofs, 4 printer's proofs
Printers: James Hughes and Robert W. Franklin
2009-61-64

72
Jules Olitski (American, born Russia, 1922–2007)
The Grey, 1988
Color offset lithograph and screenprint, numbered 50/90
Image/sheet: 21¹⁵/₁₆ x 30¹/₁₆ inches (55.7 x 76.4 cm)
Edition: 90, 20 artist's proofs
Printers: James Hughes and Robert W. Franklin (offset lithograph)
and Allan L. Edmunds (screenprint)
2009-61-65

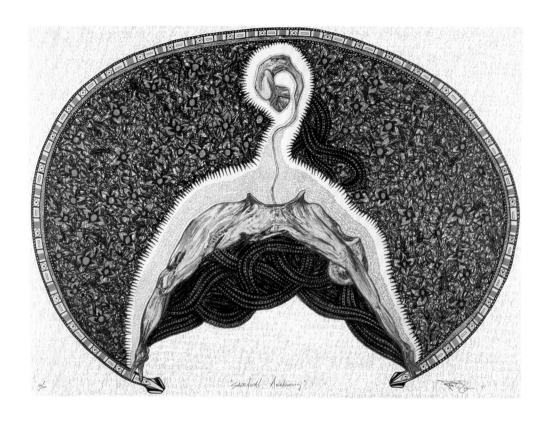

73

Pedro Ospina (Colombian, born 1964)
Sacrificial Awakening, 1991
Color offset lithograph, numbered 50/100
Image/sheet: 21⁷/₈ x 30 inches (55.6 x 76.2 cm)
Edition: 100, 20 artist's proofs, 2 printer's proofs
Printers: James Hughes and Robert W. Franklin
2009-61-66

74

Charles Parness (American, born 1945)
Fish Tales, 1989
Color offset lithograph, numbered 50/130
Image/sheet: 21⁵/₈ x 29¹¹/₁₆ inches (54.9 x 75.4 cm)
Edition: 130, 16 artist's proofs, 1 printer's proof
Printers: James Hughes and Robert W. Franklin
2009-61-67

75

Anna Marie Pavlik (American, born 1952)
Artistic Perspective, 2001
Color offset lithograph, numbered 29/30
Image (irregular): 20³/₈ x 28¹/₂ inches (51.8 x 72.4 cm)
Sheet: 22 x 29³/₄ inches (55.9 x 75.6 cm)
Edition: 30, 4 artist's proofs, 2 printer's proofs
Printer: Robert W. Franklin
2009-61-68

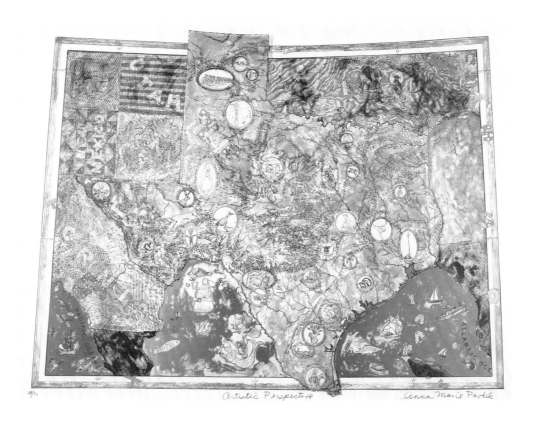

Artistic Perspective   Anna Marie Pavlik

76

Howardena Pindell (American, born 1943)

Autobiography: Past & Present, 1988–89

Color offset lithograph and screenprint diptych, numbered 20/55

Image/sheets (two joined): 21^9/$_{16}$ x 59^7/$_8$ inches (54.8 x 152.1 cm)

Edition: 55, 10 artist's proofs

Printers: Robert W. Franklin (offset lithograph) and

Allan L. Edmunds (screenprint)

2009-61-69a,b

77
Dwight Pogue (American, born 1944)
Fringed Gentian II, 1986
Color offset lithograph, numbered 32/100
Image/sheet: 30 $^{1}/_{16}$ x 21 $^{3}/_{8}$ inches (76.4 x 54.3 cm)
Edition: 100
Printers: James Hughes and Robert W. Franklin
2009-61-98

78
Valentin Popov (American, born Ukraine, born 1956)
Welcome to Nineties, 1992
Color offset lithograph, numbered 50/99
Image/sheet: 21 $^{3}/_{4}$ x 30 inches (55.2 x 76.2 cm)
Edition: 99, 48 artist's proofs, 3 printer's proofs
Printer: Robert W. Franklin
2009-61-70

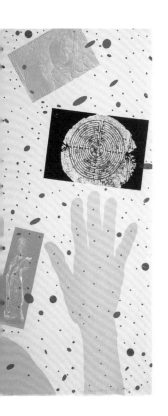

79
Alison Saar (American, born 1956)
Black Snake Blues, 1994
Color offset lithograph, numbered 50/70
Image/sheet: 21 $^{13}/_{16}$ x 29 $^{13}/_{16}$ inches (55.4 x 75.7 cm)
Edition: 70, 20 artist's proofs, 5 printer's proofs
Printer: Robert W. Franklin
2009-61-71

80
Betye Saar (American, born 1926)
Mystic Sky with Self-Portrait, 1992
Color offset lithograph with paper construction,
numbered 44/100
Image/sheet: 21 $^7/_{16}$ x 25 $^1/_4$ inches (54.5 x 64.1 cm)
Edition: 100, 10 artist's proofs, 2 printer's proofs
Printers: James Hughes and Robert W. Franklin
2009-61-72

81
Marta Sanchez (American, born 1959)
R cigarro, R barril, 2002
Color offset lithograph, numbered 44/46
Image/sheet: 29 $^{15}/_{16}$ x 21 $^{3}/_{8}$ inches (76 x 54.3 cm)
Edition: 46, 4 artist's proofs, 3 printer's proofs
Printers: James Hughes and Robert W. Franklin
2009-61-73

82
Paul Santoleri (American, born 1965)
Neither Here Nor There, 2000
Color offset lithograph, numbered 50/86
Image/sheet: 21 $^{3}/_{4}$ x 29 $^{13}/_{16}$ inches (55.2 x 75.7 cm)
Edition: 86, 4 artist's proofs, 2 printer's proofs
Printer: Robert W. Franklin
2009-61-74

83
Toshio Sasaki (Japanese, 1946–2007)
Bronx Project, 1991
Color offset lithograph, numbered 51/64
Image/sheet: 21³/₄ x 30 inches
(55.3 x 76.2 cm)
Edition: 64, 3 artist's proofs, 4 printer's proofs
Printer: Robert W. Franklin
2009-61-75

84
Judith Schaechter (American, born 1961)
Virtue Triumphs (When the Devil Sleeps), 1991
Color offset lithograph, numbered 48/50
Image/sheet: 21⁵/₁₆ x 22³/₁₆ inches
(54.1 x 56.4 cm)
Edition: 50, 20 artist's proofs, 10 printer's proofs
Printer: Robert W. Franklin
2009-61-76

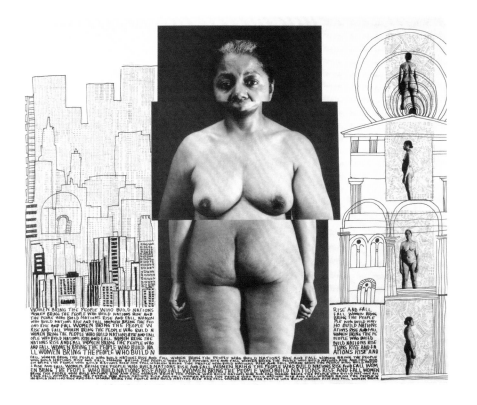

85
Clarissa Sligh (American, born 1939)
Women Bring the People, 2006
Color offset lithograph, numbered 50/60
Image: 21⁵/₁₆ x 25¹/₈ inches (54.1 x 63.8 cm)
Sheet: 21⁷/₈ x 25¹/₈ inches (55.6 x 63.8 cm)
Edition: 60, 4 artist's proofs, 3 printer's proofs
Printer: Robert W. Franklin
2009-61-77

86
Patricia M. Smith (American, born 1949)
Portrait of a Model Child, 1985
Color offset lithograph, numbered 50/100
Image: 25⁵/₈ x 18¹³/₁₆ inches (65.1 x 47.8 cm)
Sheet: 30 x 22¹/₁₆ inches (76.2 x 56 cm)
Edition: 100, 10 artist's proofs
Printers: James Hughes and Robert W. Franklin
2009-61-79

87
Vincent D. Smith (American, 1929–2003)
Jonkonnu Festival, 1996
Color offset lithograph, numbered 48/70
Image/sheet: 21⁹/₁₆ x 29³/₄ inches (54.8 x 75.6 cm)
Edition: 70, 14 artist's proofs, 4 printer's proofs
Printers: James Hughes and Robert W. Franklin
2009-61-80

88
Edgar Sorrells-Adewale (American, born 1936)
The Laying On of Hands Is a Time Honored Ritual, 1997
Color offset lithograph, numbered 50/100
Image/sheet: 29⁵/₈ x 21¹/₂ inches (75.2 x 54.6 cm)
Edition: 100, 20 artist's proofs, 4 printer's proofs
Printers: James Hughes and Robert W. Franklin
2009-61-81

89
Lori Spencer (American, born 1963)
Three Fates at the Edge of the Garden of Eden, 1997
Color offset lithograph, numbered 50/100
Image/sheet: 21¹/₄ x 29³/₄ inches (54 x 75.6 cm)
Edition: 100, 20 artist's proofs, 4 printer's proofs
Printers: James Hughes and Robert W. Franklin
2009-61-82

90
Vuyile Voyiya (South African, born 1961)
Blissfull Swing III, 2007
Linocut, numbered 4/10
Block: 23³/₄ x 34⁷/₈ inches (60.3 x 88.6 cm)
Sheet: 30¹/₈ x 42⁵/₈ inches (76.5 x 108.2 cm)
Edition: 10, 1 artist's proof
Printer: Vuyile Voyiya
2009-61-94

91
Larry Walker (American, born 1935)
Saguaro Spirits—Visitors, 2001
Color offset lithograph, numbered 8/48
Image/sheet: 21 1/2 x 29 3/16 inches (54.6 x 74.1 cm)
Edition: 48, 6 artist's proofs, 3 printer's proofs
Printer: Robert W. Franklin
2009-61-83

92
Kay WalkingStick (Native American, born 1935)
Onrush of Time, 1990
Color offset lithograph triptych, unnumbered
Image/sheets (three joined): 20 x 47 7/8 inches
(50.8 x 121.6 cm)
Edition: 50, 20 artist's proofs
Printer: Robert W. Franklin
2009-61-84a–c

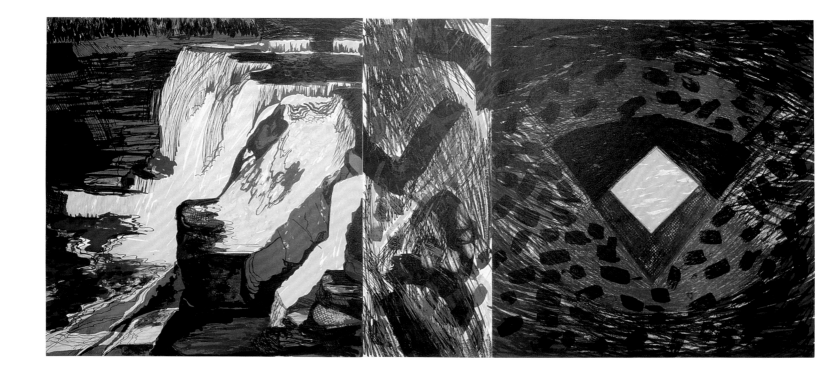

93
James Lesesne Wells (American, 1902–1993)
Phoenix Ascending, 1985
Color offset lithograph, numbered 62/100
Image: 27 x 20 $\frac{5}{8}$ inches (68.6 x 52.4 cm)
Sheet: 29 $\frac{3}{4}$ x 21 $\frac{15}{16}$ inches (75.6 x 55.7 cm)
Edition: 100
Printer: Robert W. Franklin
2009-61-85

94
William T. Williams (American, born 1942)
Time of Song, 2005
Color offset lithograph, numbered 4/60
Image: 15 $\frac{1}{2}$ x 22 $\frac{5}{16}$ inches (39.4 x 56.7 cm)
Sheet: 19 $\frac{1}{4}$ x 26 $\frac{1}{16}$ inches (48.9 x 66.2 cm)
Edition: 60, 6 artist's proofs, 5 printer's proofs
Printer: Robert W. Franklin
2009-61-86

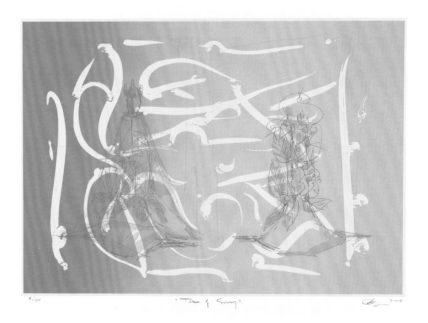

95
Wucius Wong (Chinese, born 1936)
Towards Enlightenment A (Yellow), 1991
Color offset lithograph, numbered 50/75
Image/sheet: 30 x 21³/₄ inches (76.2 x 55.2 cm)
Edition: 75, 31 artist's proofs, 1 printer's proof
Printers: James Hughes and Robert W. Franklin
2009-61-87

96
Wucius Wong
Towards Enlightenment B (Green), 1991
Color offset lithograph, numbered 50/60
Image/sheet: 30 x 21⁹/₁₆ inches (76.2 x 54.8 cm)
Edition: 60
Printer: Robert W. Franklin
2009-61-88

97
Kathryn Jo Yarrington (American, born 1950)
Moving Day, 1987
Color offset lithograph, numbered 50/100
Image/sheet: 21^5/$_8$ x 29^{15}/$_{16}$ inches (54.9 x 76 cm)
Edition: 100, 1 artist's proof
Printer: Robert W. Franklin
2009-61-89

98
Isaiah Zagar (American, born 1939)
Isaiah, 1986
Color offset lithograph, numbered 38/100
Image/sheet: 29^{15}/$_{16}$ x 21^3/$_4$ inches (76 x 55.2 cm)
Edition: 100, 20 artist's proofs
Printer: Robert W. Franklin
2009-61-90

99
Alexander Zakharov (Russian, born 1960)
The Bird, 1995
Color offset lithograph, numbered 50/82
Image: 21 3/4 x 29 3/4 inches (55.2 x 75.6 cm)
Sheet: 22 1/8 x 29 3/4 inches (56.2 x 75.6 cm)
Edition: 82, 23 artist's proofs, 4 printer's proofs
Printer: Robert W. Franklin
2009-61-91

100
Murray Zimiles (American, born 1941)
Two Dogs, 1998
Color offset lithograph, numbered 60/60
Image/sheet: 21 5/8 x 29 7/8 inches
(54.9 x 75.9 cm)
Edition: 60, 6 artist's proofs, 2 printer's proofs
Printers: James Hughes and Robert W. Franklin
2009-61-92

Chronology

Shelley R. Langdale

1948

Artist Robert Blackburn founds the nonprofit Printmaking Workshop in New York, creating an egalitarian environment in which artists of all ages, backgrounds, and expertise are encouraged to use both traditional and experimental techniques.

Philadelphia printmaker Eugene Feldman establishes Falcon Press; his innovative use of offset lithography for fine art prints opens new possibilities for the medium.

1957–66

A printmaking renaissance is set off by the creation of a number of print workshops across the United States, beginning with Universal Limited Art Editions in New York and followed by workshops in Los Angeles, San Francisco, and elsewhere (see p. 21 n. 7).

1960

Prints in Progress, a program of printmaking demonstrations by local artists in Philadelphia public schools, is started by the Print Club (now the Print Center).

1965

The National Endowment for the Arts granting agency is established by the United States Congress to support a wide variety of art institutions.

1966

Freedom Theatre, Pennsylvania's oldest African American theater and one of the city's first ethnic-centered art groups, is founded in Philadelphia.

1968

Artist Lou Stovall opens his printmaking facility, Workshop Inc., in Washington, D.C.

In the wake of Dr. Martin Luther King's assassination, activists poured into Philadelphia to attend a Black Power Conference, protesting racism and promoting black unity, self-determination, and civil rights issues.

1969

The controversial photography exhibition *Harlem on My Mind* opens at the Metropolitan Museum of Art in New York. The exclusion of African Americans from its planning, and its documentary approach, including the decision not to show paintings or other works of art by contemporary black artists, creates a surge in activism to push mainstream art institutions to exhibit this work. Artists Benny Andrews and Henri Ghent form the Black Emergency Cultural Coalition (BECC).

The exhibition *Afro-American Artists, 1800–1969*, organized by the Division of Art Education of the School District of Philadelphia, is held at the Philadelphia Civic Center.

1970

Philadelphia Dance Company (PHILADANCO) is founded and will become internationally celebrated for its innovation as well as its preservation of predominantly African American traditions in dance.

1971

Philadelphian Allan Edmunds, having just completed his degree at Temple University's Tyler School of Art, visits Blackburn's Print-making Workshop in New York, which inspires him to consider setting up a printmaking facility in Philadelphia.

Edmunds is commissioned to create a print and poster for the exhibition *Silkscreen: History of a Medium* at the Philadelphia Museum of Art.

1972

Young Philadelphia-based printmakers, including John E. Dowell, Jr., Phyllis Thompson, James Gadson, and Allan Edmunds, continue to gain recognition, increasing interest in the medium within the city's minority community. The enrollment of minority students at Philadelphia art colleges is also increasing dramatically.

Brandywine Graphic Workshop opens in October at 1923 Brandywine Street—previously occupied by one of the Print Club's Prints in Progress workshops—in the racially diverse Fairmount neighborhood in North Philadelphia. The mission quickly expands from training young artists and local high school students to also providing opportunities for serious artists of all ages and ethnicities to create original prints in a collaborative setting. Founding artist Allan Edmunds serves as master printer.

1974

Taller Puertorriqueño is established by Latino artists and activists in the North Kensington area of Philadelphia as a community-based graphic-arts workshop providing cultural training alternatives to local youth and promoting the arts as a vehicle for social change.

Brandywine Graphic Workshop (aka Brandywine Workshop) is incorporated as a nonprofit 501(c)3 organization.

Fig. 15. Sam Gilliam at Brandywine Workshop during his tenure as the first visiting artist-in-residence, 1975

1975

Abstract painter Sam Gilliam, a key figure in the Washington [D.C.] Color School movement, is the first visiting artist-in-residence at Brandywine Workshop.

The workshop receives its first grant award from the Pennsylvania Council on the Arts and uses it to provide a residency for Romare Bearden.

1976

Brandywine Workshop inaugurates the Van Der Zee Award for Visual Artists, named after the Harlem-based photographer James Van Der Zee. First presented to Romare Bearden, the award is given to distinguished African American artists in recognition of their talent and their contributions to broadening opportunities for artists of color; the recipient creates a print at the workshop the year he or she is honored.

Brandywine Workshop begins to donate "satellite collections" of its prints to public institutions and universities—beginning with the National Collection of Fine Arts (now the Smithsonian American Art Museum) in Washington, D.C.—to ensure wide access to the work and expand the institutions' holdings of art by culturally diverse contemporary artists (see p. 21 n. 30).

1977

Marion Boulton Stroud founds the Fabric Workshop in Philadelphia, dedicated to inviting experimentation among leading contemporary artists and to sharing the artistic process with the public through a variety of educational programs, including apprenticeships for Philadelphia high school students.

A four-story loft building at 1520–22 Kater Street in Philadelphia is purchased by Anne and Allan Edmunds, and the first two floors are designated to replace Brandywine Workshop's increasingly cramped facility on Brandywine Street.

The workshop's artist residency program is put on hiatus during the three-year renovation of the the Kater Street space. In the interim, Brandywine inaugurates the Visual Artists in Public Service (VAPS) program and focuses its activities on educational outreach, partnering with local organizations and drawing on local and national funding sources, such as the federal government's Comprehensive Employment and Training Act (CETA); projects include painting murals, creating gardens (art parks), outdoor performances, and instruction in various art mediums in low-income neighborhoods.

1980
The artist residency program resumes in the completed Kater Street facility with Chicago sculptor and Van Der Zee Award recipient Richard Hunt (see plate 48).

Brandywine's "Philly Panache" program continues its projects intended to engage artists in public service and bring art to inner-city neighborhoods, after its VAPS program ends with the cessation of support through CETA.

1982
Brandywine switches its main focus from screenprinting to offset lithography with the acquisition of a single-color offset litho press, establishing its Offset Institute.

1983
Robert Blackburn receives Brandywine's first Lifetime Achievement Award, given to an educator, historian, civic leader, artist, or arts patron to honor his or her commitment to artists and to improving the community through the arts.

A two-color offset lithography press is acquired for the workshop. James Hughes is hired as master offset printer.

1984
Mayor W. Wilson Goode adds a mural component (now the Mural Arts Program) to the Philadelphia Anti-Graffiti Network, hiring artist Jane Golden to reach out to graffiti writers and redirect their energies toward mural painting.

1986
Brandywine's first traveling exhibition, *Contemporary Print Images: Works by Afro-American Artists from the Brandywine Workshop*, is organized by the Smithsonian Institution Traveling Exhibition Service for a four-year, forty-two-site tour across the United States.

James Hughes trains Robert Franklin to assist him at the workshop. Franklin becomes lead pressman and eventually replaces Hughes as master offset printer.

Brandywine sponsors the exhibition *Hispanic Artists Prints from Bob Blackburn's Printmaking Workshop*, hosted by Taller Puertorriqueño in Philadelphia.

1987
The exhibition *USA Printworks: Selections from the Brandywine Workshop Collection* begins a tour of Africa, the first of several Brandywine exhibitions over the next decade to travel abroad under the auspices of the United States Information Agency's Arts America Program.

The British American Arts Association initiates a visual-arts exchange between communities in Philadelphia and Wales. The resulting artist residencies yield a Brandywine mural project (1991) and the exhibition *Collaborations: Printmaking in Philadelphia*, featuring prints created at six Philadelphia-based institutions—Brandywine Workshop, The Fabric Workshop, The University of the Arts, C. R. Ettinger Studio, Franz Spohn–Why Not Print?, and Corridor Press—held at the Glynn Vivian Art Gallery in Swansea, Wales, in 1989.

Fig. 16. Eleanor Childs, an administrator at Brandywine Workshop, Dr. Francis Musango, head of the School of Fine Arts, Makerere University, Uganda, and Allan Edmunds at Brandywine Workshop's exhibition *USA Printworks: Selections from the Brandywine Workshop Collection*, which traveled to Makerere University in June 1988

1988
The Borowsky Center for Publication Arts is established at the University of the Arts in Philadelphia under the leadership of faculty Lois M. Johnson and Patricia Smith, both members of Brandywine's Artist Advisory Committee.

Brandywine's residency program focuses on outreach to Native American artists, six of whom give talks at the Print Club in Philadelphia through 1989.

1989
Brandywine Workshop organizes an exhibition of its prints by visiting artists, *African American Abstraction in Printmaking*, which travels to Los Angeles, San Diego, Newark (New Jersey), Atlanta, New Orleans, and Chicago over the next two years.

Fig. 17. Wucius Wong at work on his print *Towards Enlightenment B (Green)* (see plate 96), Brandywine Workshop, 1991

1991
Several parcels of properties, vacant lots, and abandoned buildings are acquired by the workshop for development into a mini-campus for the visual arts that will contribute to the expansion of Philadelphia's Avenue of the Arts Cultural District along South Broad Street.

1993
Brandywine's Firehouse Art Center opens in a refurbished historic firehouse at 730–32 South Broad Street. It includes room for educational programs in computer graphics and video and the workshop's first designated exhibition space, the Printed Image Gallery.

Sam Gilliam: Recent Monoprints, the first all-print exhibition of the artist's work, is one of two inaugural exhibitions at the Printed Image Gallery; the other, *Philadelphia Printmakers*, surveys the prints of Philadelphia-based artists who have worked at Brandywine since its inception.

Diverseworks: Diez años de grabados de Taller Brandywine, an exhibition organized by Brandywine Workshop, embarks on a multination tour of Latin America.

1994
The exhibition *Signs & Symbols: Communication and Interpretation from the Brandywine Workshop* is sent on a two-year tour of Middle and Near Eastern nations.

Latin and Latin American Artist Prints, an exhibition featuring prints from the Brandywine Workshop, Self Help Graphics (Los Angeles), and Lehigh University (Bethlehem, Pennsylvania) is held at the Printed Image Gallery.

1995

The first exhibition featuring Benny Andrews's prints, *Benny Andrews: Chronicles and Recollections*, is organized by and shown at Brandywine Workshop.

1996–97

Brandywine's artist residency program focuses on artists of Asian heritage, resulting in two exhibitions in its Printed Image Gallery, *Inside/Out: Japanese and Japanese American Artist Prints* and *Impressions: Contemporary Asian Artist Prints*.

Allan Edmunds begins a series of trips to Cuba with Ricardo Viera, director of Lehigh University Art Galleries, to explore possibilities for artist exchanges.

Fig. 18. Robert Blackburn dancing at the dedication of the new Brandywine Workshop building at 728 South Broad Street, Philadelphia, 1997

1997

Brandywine's printmaking facilities are moved from Kater Street to a newly constructed building at 728 South Broad Street, adjacent to the Firehouse Art Center. The old presses are replaced by a larger-format DUFA flatbed offset litho press. Photo-screenprinting and relief printing continue to be offered as alternative techniques.

1999

Four Cuban artists—José Omar Torres, Ibrahim Miranda, Belkis Ayón, and Choco (Eduardo Roca Salazar)—participate in residencies organized by Brandywine Workshop at its facility and at the Tyler School of Art (Temple University) and the University of the Arts in Philadelphia.

2000

Hidden Images: Contemporary Cuban Graphic Art, a two-site exhibition of works produced during Brandywine's Cuban artist residency program and of loans from Cuban artists, is held at the workshop's Printed Image Gallery and at Taller Puertorriqueño.

Diverseworks (Revisited), an exhibition of prints from Brandywine Workshop, is held at the Palacio del Segundo Cabo in Havana. As part of the Havana Biennial, Brandywine runs a printmaking workshop sponsored by Havana's Wifredo Lam Contemporary Art Center and the Experimental Graphics Workshop.

Philadelphia Print Collaborative (later renamed Philagrafika), a consortium of printmaking workshops, artists, printmaking professors, and curators of local print collections, is founded by Robert Brand. Allan Edmunds serves on the board, and Brandywine Workshop is a key supporter of the effort to unite the marketing and programming of various print organizations.

2001

Brandywine Workshop launches an initiative to host residencies by artists working in southern states. An exhibition of the resulting works, *Southern Exposure*, is held at the Printed Image Gallery and travels to the University of Little Rock, Arkansas.

2002

The exhibition *African American Presence in American Printmaking (Historic Prints from Private Collections)* is held in Brandywine's Printed Image Gallery.

Fig. 19. Artist Benny Andrews (left) and pressman Marion Beaufort at the offset lithography press, Brandywine Workshop, 2004

2004

The book *Three Decades of American Printmaking: The Brandywine Workshop Collection* is published by Hudson Hills Press.

2006

The workshop launches its "American Cities" exhibition series, showcasing contemporary works on paper made by African American artists in particular regions. Artists from Houston (2006) and Detroit (2008) are featured before the program ends with the closing of the Printed Image Gallery.

2008

The Firehouse Art Center of Brandywine Workshop, along with its Printed Image Gallery, is closed for restoration and renovations, and all of Brandywine's operations are moved to 728 South Broad Street, where the lobby is used for small installations.

2009

One hundred prints from the Brandywine Workshop are donated to the Philadelphia Museum of Art in memory of its former director Anne d'Harnoncourt.

2011

Brandywine receives donations of prints from the Estate of Robert W. Blackburn and the Printmaking Workshop, and from Camille Billops and the Hatch-Billops Collection in New York, greatly enhancing the breadth and diversity of its permanent collection of contemporary prints in all mediums.

The exhibition *Infinite Mirror: Images of American Identity*, conceived by Brandywine Workshop and implemented by International Art & Artists (Washington, D.C.) and Artrain (Ann Arbor, Michigan), and which includes a selection of Brandywine prints, begins a national tour.

2012

Brandywine Workshop celebrates its fortieth anniversary, having produced some eight hundred editioned prints by nearly three hundred artists. New initiatives designed to serve young artists are launched, including efforts to make the workshop's archives, educational resources, and videos of artist interviews available online and to prepare traveling exhibitions of works from the permanent collection.

Fig. 20. Exterior view of the Brandywine Workshop at 728 South Broad Street, Philadelphia, 2012

Glossary of Printmaking Terms

Edition: The total number of impressions printed from the same block, plate, stone, or screen. This does not typically include artists' proofs and other proofs considered "outside" the edition (see "proofs," below). Edition size is generally designated on each print as a fraction: in an edition size of one hundred prints the works will be numbered individually, from 1/100 through 100/100.

Lithograph: A print created by drawing an image with crayon or another greasy medium on a stone slab or a metal (often aluminum) plate. The stone or plate is kept damp when the greasy printing ink is applied (making use of the fact that grease repels water), so that the ink adheres only to the greasy areas to be printed. The inked image is then transferred to paper when the stone or plate is run through the printing press.

Offset lithograph: A print made using a lithographic plate in which the inked image is transferred (offset) onto the smooth rubber cylinder of an offset printing press, which in turn transfers the image from the cylinder onto a sheet of paper. The resulting image thus retains the original orientation of the image created on the initial lithographic plate (since it is reversed onto the cylinder and then reversed again when transferred to the paper), unlike most printing techniques, in which the image is reversed only once during printing.

Proofs: Additional impressions of a print, outside the official edition. These are designated for use by the artist, printer, or publisher, often as compensation for their contributions to the project, or as a courtesy.

Screenprint: A form of stenciled printing in which the stenciled image is adhered to a fine-mesh screen (fixed tautly on a frame). The screen is laid face down on a sheet of paper, and printing ink is spread over the screen and forced through the open areas of the mesh with a squeegee (rubber blade), transferring the image to the paper underneath. The image can be applied to the screen in various ways, using masking stencils made of paper or gelatin (including photomechanically produced film) or by painting out areas of the screen with a liquid that sets and blocks holes in the mesh.

Woodcut or linocut: A print made from a design cut in a block of wood or linoleum. The image is drawn on the flat block, and the areas around each line of the design are cut away with a gouge or sharp knife so that the lines stand out in relief, ready to be inked using a dauber or roller. The ink is transferred from the raised surfaces of the lines to paper through pressure applied either by hand, using a spoon or other implement to rub the back of the sheet laid on top of the block, or by using a printing press.

Selected Bibliography

Listed chronologically

Edmunds, Allan L., and Keith Morrison. *Contemporary Print Images: Works by Afro-American Artists from the Brandywine Workshop.* Washington, D.C.: Smithsonian Institution Traveling Exhibition Service, 1986.

Morrison, Keith. *USA Printworks: Selections from the Brandywine Workshop Collection.* Text in English and French. Exh. cat. [under the auspices of the Arts in America Program of the United States Information Agency]. Philadelphia: Brandywine Workshop, 1987.

Beardsley, John, and David Stephens. *Sam Gilliam: Recent Monoprints.* Exh. cat. Philadelphia: Brandywine Workshop, 1993.

Courtney, Julie. *Diverseworks: Diez años de grabados de Taller Brandywine.* Exh. cat. [under the auspices of the Arts in America Program of the United States Information Agency]. Text in Spanish. Philadelphia: Brandywine Workshop, 1994.

Williams, William E. *Signs & Symbols: Communication and Interpretation from Brandywine Workshop.* Text in English and Arabic. Exh. cat. [under the auspices of the Arts in America Program of the United States Information Agency]. Philadelphia: Brandywine Workshop, [c. 1994].

Edmunds, Allan L. *Benny Andrews: Chronicles and Recollections.* Exh. cat. Philadelphia: Brandywine Workshop, 1995.

Williams, William E. *John Dowell: Three Moments in Time; A Survey of Prints, 1970–1995.* Exh. cat. Philadelphia: Brandywine Workshop, 1995.

Stein, Judith E. *Jacob Landau: Old Man Mad About Drawing; Works on Paper, 1934–1995.* Exh. cat. Philadelphia: Brandywine Workshop, 1996.

Lee, Robert. *Impressions: Contemporary Asian Artist Prints.* Exh. cat. Philadelphia: Brandywine Workshop, 1997.

Machida, Margo. *Inside/Out: Japanese and Japanese American Artist Prints.* Exh. cat. Philadelphia: Brandywine Workshop, 1997.

Edmunds, Allan L., Sande Webster, and Lewis Tanner Moore. *Paul Keene: Serial Images; Prints, Drawings, Mixed Media, and Collages.* Exh. cat. Philadelphia: Brandywine Workshop, 1998.

Taha, Halima, et al. *Three Decades of American Printmaking: The Brandywine Workshop Collection.* New York: Hudson Hills, 2004.

Bradford, Blake, Benito Huerta, and Robert Lee. *Infinite Mirror: Images of American Identity.* Exh. cat. Washington, D.C.: International Art and Artists; Ann Arbor, Mich.: Artrain, 2011.